The Return
of
Hijâb

Part II

Compiled and edited by:
Muhammad Ahmad Isma'eel Al-Muqaddam

Al-Firdous Ltd, London.

2002: First Edition.

Translated by Abdallah Elaceri.
Typeset by Abu Yusuf

ISBN 1 874263 90 6

Published and Distributed by:
Al-Firdous Ltd
10 Fonthill Road
London
N4 3HX

www.al-firdous.co.uk

Email: books@al-firdous.co.uk

Printed and Bound by :
Deluxe Printers, London NW10 7NR
Tel : 020 8965 1771

I ask Allah ﷻ to accept this translation effort of the second part of

"The Return of Hijab" which I dedicate to my fiancée "Rkia" (Ruqayyah)

Table of Contents

Introduction

Praise to Allah alone; I praise Him with a lasting praise, and I thank Him for all His unlimited Graces. I testify that there is no god worthy of worship but Allah alone with no associated partners, and I testify that Muhammad ﷺ is His Messenger and the last of His prophets. He ﷺ chose him, brought him close to Him, loved him, praised him, honored him and elevated him above all the rest ﷺ.

Every sincere faithful person is aware of the situation of Islam and the Muslims, which has eventually resulted in their strangeness in this world; those who follow the teachings of Islam are few, and those who transgress form the majority. The regulations of many legislations have or may have been discarded, which has led to the spreading of Fitna[1] and its dire consequences for the majority of people; it confirmed the Hadith of the Prophet ﷺ: "Islam will be discarded the way the embroidery of an old fabric disappears, until there would be no knowledge of Salat, Siyam (Fasting), Sadaqah, and other forms of ritual worship"[2], and he ﷺ said: "Islam initiated as something strange, and it would revert to its (old position) of being strange; so, good tidings for the

---

[1] Fitnah (plural: Fitan) civil strife, sedition, schism, trial, temptation. Examples of fitnah: Shirk (Associating something or someone to Allah ﷻ), spread of vice and immorality in society, etc…

[2] Part of Hadith transmitted by Ibn Maajah, Al-Hakim in "Al-Mustadrak", Al-Baihaqui in "Ashi'ab" and Ad-Dayya' on the authority of Hudhaifah ﷺ; it has an authentic chain of authorities, and its narrators are trustworthy.

strangers"[1]. In another narration, the Companions ﷺ asked: "And who are the strangers?" the Prophet ﷺ replied: "Those who do good deeds when people live in depravity."[2]

Abdullah bin Amru bin Al-'Aas ﷺ reported that the Prophet ﷺ said: "Good tidings for the strangers", so they said: "Who are they O Messenger of Allah?" he ﷺ replied: "Some good people among many bad people; those who disobey them outnumber those who obey them"[3]; and in another narration "Those who hate them outnumber those who love them". Anas bin Malik ﷺ reported that the Prophet ﷺ said: "There will come a time when, for those people who persevere and hold on to their Deen, it would be like holding tightly to a hot piece of coal"[4].

Al-Manawi said: "The Prophet ﷺ likened the reasonable with the perceptible; i.e. the one who holds tight to the regulations of the Book and the Sunnah, endures all sorts of ill treatment from the people who went astray and innovated in Islam; his suffering is similar to the person who handles fire and touches it, yet it might be even harder. This was one of the miracles of the Prophet ﷺ;

---

[1] Transmitted by Muslim in the chapter of Iman in his Sahih book, on the authority of Abu Hurairah ﷺ.
[2] Transmitted by Attabarani and Abu Nasr in "Al-Ibanah", on the authority of Abdurahman bin Sunnah.
[3] Transmitted by Imam Ahmad, and Al-Haithami said: "Its authority includes ibn Lahee'ah whose narration is weak".
[4] Transmitted by Attirmidhi who said that this particular narration is strange. However, Imam Assuyuti thought it was a sound narration.

that he could inform us about the unknown, which has, indeed, taken place".

Al-Mubarakfuri said: "Attayibi said, explaining the Hadith: "Just as one who holds a hot piece of coal would not hold it long enough to burn his hands, likewise, the religious (conservative) person would not be able to hold tight to his Deen, because of the predominance of sins and sinners, the spreading of immorality, and the weakness of Iman"[1].

Ibn Mas'oud ﷺ reported that the Prophet ﷺ said: "After you, there will a be time of patience, the one who perseveres in it will get the reward of fifty of among you"[2].

Abu Umamah Sha'baani said: "I asked Abu Tha'labah Al-Khushany ﷺ: 'What do you say regarding the Verse: ❨You are only responsible for yourselves❩'? He said: 'By Allah! I have asked a well informed person, I asked the Prophet ﷺ who replied: 'Enjoin one another to do what is reputable and forbid one another from doing what is disreputable. But when you see niggardliness being obeyed, passion being followed, worldly interests being preferred, everyone being charmed by his own opinion, and you will see something you are inclined to do, caring only for yourself, ignoring what people, in general, are doing; for ahead of you are days which will require endurance, in which he who shows endurance will be like

---

[1] From "Tuhfat Al-Ahwadi" (6/539).
[2] Transmitted by Attabarani in Al-Kabir (3/79/1) and it was authenticated by Al-Albani.

11

him who grasps red hot coals. The one who acts rightly during that period will have the reward of fifty men who act as he does.'"[1] Abu Dawud added in his narration: The hearers said, "Is that the reward of fifty of us or of them, O Messenger of Allah?" He ﷺ replied, "The reward of fifty of you."

Ma'qil bin Yasar ◉ said: the Prophet ﷺ said: "Worshipping during a period of widespread turmoil is like emigration towards me"[2]; i.e. worshipping during the time of Fitnah is like an emigration towards the Prophet ﷺ. An-Nawawi, Allah's Grace upon him, said: "The great merit of the worship in those particular times is that most people will neglect it and disregard it, but only some individuals will devote their time to it"[3].

Al-Hafidh bin Hajar, Allah's Grace upon him, said: "Explaining the term 'turmoil' in the previous Hadith, Imam Ahmad and Attabarani transmitted a sound Hadith, on the authority of Khalid bin Al-Waleed ◉, that a man told him: O Abu Sulaiman! Fear Allah, for Fitan have appeared, he said: 'As long as Al-Khattab is alive, there won't be any, however, it would take place after him, and the man would seek any place away from Fitnah, but will not find a safe one; those are the days mentioned by the Prophet ﷺ, which will be the days of turmoil close to the Hour."

---

[1] Transmitted by Attirmidhi, Abudawud and Ibn Majah
[2] Transmitted by Muslim and Attirmidhi.
[3] An-Nawawi in his book interpreting Sahih Muslim (18/88).

A Woman is a Weapon with Two Sharp Ends

As the earth was at its loveliest and took on its fairest guise... and its people thought they had it under their control...

Many people disregarded their Deen and followed the temptations of life; they were seduced by western civilization and eastern adornments, and all this coincided with the absence of those who call people to the right path, and the scholars – apart from some, who were blessed by Allah ﷻ – who concealed the Revelations of Allah. The enemies of Islam have not neglected us; they have set out their invasion, armed with the poisonous arrows of desire and suspicion, to damage the hearts of the Muslims, explore their homes, and strip them of the Deen that Allah ﷻ Had chosen for them...

Those enemies were sly and vicious in their war against the Muslims; they identified and specified the reasons behind the power of the Muslims, and worked hard to base and destroy them, using all malicious means...

They realized that women were among the greatest most powerful assets in the Islamic society, and they also knew that she could become a weapon with two sharp ends; that she was liable to be the most efficient means of creating Fitnah and destruction. Therefore, they paid a great deal of attention to herin the balance of their conspiracies to bring down the Caliphate, which came to

13

an abrupt end, having flags of the "star of David" flapping over Islamic capitals[1].

Muhammad Tal'at Harb said, in his book, "The Education of Women and Hijab": "There is no obstacle preventing the destruction of the Islamic society in the East – not only in Egypt – lest Muslim women undertake a change...for depravity has spread among men in the East"[2]. Women possess some great talents by which she is able to build a nation or destroy it; Abu Sa'id Al-Khudri ؓ stated that, the Prophet ﷺ said: "The world is sweet and green (alluring) and verily Allah is going to install you as vicegerent in it in order to see how you act. So avoid the allurement of women: Verily, the first trial for the people of Israel was caused by women"[3]. Usamah bin Zaid and Sa'id bin Zaid ؓ said: 'The Prophet ﷺ said: "After me, I have not left an affliction more harmful to men than women"[4].

Muslim women have played a vital role in building the Islamic Structure; the whole Islamic nation has benefited

---

[1] And did you know about the incident that took place during the time of the Uthomani Sultan, Abdulhamid; he had ordered the re-building of Al-Quds (Jerusalem) in 1860, and the assigned City Governor, Kamil Basha, had authorized for the flags of some foreign countries to be risen above their consulates, on the grounds that they had fought alongside Turkey against Russia, so the people of the city of Al-Quds revolted against him, and forced him to withdraw his authorisation, so immediately all the flags were taken down!.

[2] "Women's Movements in the East", p.11.

[3] Transmitted by Muslim – see "The interpretation of An-Nawawi" (17/55).

[4] Transmitted by Al-Bukhari, Attirmidhi, and Ibn Maajah. See "Fath Al-Bari" (9/138)

a great deal from this (sharp) side of a woman's weapon, throughout the blessed centuries. But then, it did not take long before the situation gradually deteriorated; for it was the turn of the other destructive side of a woman's weapon to injure the nation. None of us would ever come to forget the destructive role the maids had played in demolishing the high structure of the nation during its prosperous times, and we do not forget that the deviation of woman (or subjecting her to deviation) had always been the first reason behind the fall of great civilizations, whose people were inflicted with divine punishment, famine and incurable diseases, as was the case of the ancient Greeks, Romans, Persians, Indians, Babylonians, and people from other kingdoms. As for our present time, the modern age has many examples, which help to enhance the belief of the Muslim about the danger of committing those sins and pursuing those desires that westerners have indulged in, which were adopted by many a nation. Therefore, this matter is one of serious concern, and we are duly right to ask ourselves:

"What do we learn when we hear, for example, that France, the country which raises the flag of immorality, had knelt down before its enemies, surrendering with astonishing speed[1], and were scolded by their army commander, Marshal Pétain: O my people! Weigh your sins, they are heavy; you did not want to have children, you have abandoned family life, you have discarded virtue and all the spiritual morals, and you have rushed

---

[1] With reference to France defeat against the Germans in the Second World War.

15

seeking your desires, anywhere, so look to see which destiny those desires have led you to."

And we are also right to wonder and ask: "Was it not appropriate for the West to perceive the warning in the fates of those nations, which were the first to worship the physical form of women? Has you not heard of the fate of the Greeks and the Romans who were the closest to the predecessors?"

The Warning from "Pompeii[1]"

History has informed us of the perishing of this city within minutes of the sudden eruption of Vesuvius volcano, but it has not reported anything about it, except that it was a centre of the Italian Art, until Allah ﷻ decided to expose its reality, and guided some men to disclose it from within the ashes; the outcome was profound and amazing that the bodies of a whole population were preserved as stoned casts; and nothing has changed in that instant in the city, even the baker was still holding a wooden tool used to extract freshly baked bread, the drunkards were seen with their drinks to their mouths, and even the adulterous were caught uncompromising and disgraceful situations.

---

[1] Pompeii: An ancient city in western Italy, southeast of Naples, near the volcano of Vesuvius, was a city with 100.000 inhabitants, and a place where the rich Romans spent their times indulged in their desires…The life of the city came to an end following an eruption of Mount Vesuvius in 79 C.E. The city lay buried for centuries beneath several metres of volcanic ash until excavations of the site began in 1748, when it was discovered by a peasant.

16

The great lesson of "Pompeii" is what the tourists may see depicted on the entrances of some castles: scales painted on the walls; in one scale, there is a pile of jewelry, and in the other their "symbol of adultery", which had inclined the balance of the scale, to indicate that "lust" was indeed more important in their lives.

Examples of destiny of communities have not ended, on earth; nations of transgressors have perished; they were drowned, or demolished, or perished through famine, or were simply crushed. The punishment of such nations is ongoing, it has not ceased, and it will not[1]... Otherwise, why do these earthquakes strike so many people? And why do floods wash away towns and villages in both the east and west? And why do devastating diseases invade man, everywhere, while science remains helpless trying to prevent them?

As for the distortion, it is prevalent in our time; most people have been transformed into robots, having no loyalty, no compassion, nor sense of justice ...it is as if the whole of the earth is on top of a volcano!

Fitan[2] comes from Europe

The West alone is not responsible for the spreading of *fahishah*[3], in both the old and modern worlds; many nations were involved, however, the West remains more responsible for the predominance of depravity, and the

---

[1] See "Fath Al-Bari" (2/184), (8/292-293), (10/56)

[2] Plural form of Fitna (trial, temptation, civil strive..)

[3] Something obscene, abominable, or immoral, such as adultery...

17

casting of its shadows all over the world, in our time; for it has used its sciences and its talents to propagate this immorality, making it look beautiful and acceptable in the eyes of the easily duped people, especially in the east.

The West was perhaps happier for its success in having corrupted and perverted our individual morals, than for having exhausted our wealth in its products of luxury, as was declared by the American missionary, Pierre de Dodge, when he said in a lecture about Islam: "… it seems to me that Hollywood has had more effect on the present Muslim generation than their religious schools."[1]

We, Arabs – quite disgracefully – we have played our part in the propagation of all these evil deeds, in both older and modern times, and depravity is the same, whether related to the East or West. For example, when a fire attacks a house, no one asks: Where it started, before great effort is made to extinguish it. So, when we refer to the West, in our speech regarding the dangers of the disintegration of morals, as witnessed these days, we simply intend to point to the big loophole that should be closed in order to control the danger, and we have to learn a lesson from our painful past, when people used to disregard such depravities. But I they left them to pile up together until they became a set of streams overwhelming our banks; we surrendered our huge heritage in both the east and west, becoming an easy prey for the wild Tartars, Spanish fanatics and Crusaders.

---

[1] "Meditations on Woman and Society", by Muhammad Al-Majdoub.

It is not being loyal to our Deen nor our Ummah to let transgressors plant their mines in our "moral stronghold" with the intention of transforming our youth into "elements of failure", neither is it wise to let "female artists" play the same role performed by the "maids" of the older times in demolishing the structure of a nation, by corrupting its youth with luring worldly deception.

The sons of the Tartars, Crusaders and Romans were aware that among the greatest help that our ancestors had, in their conquest of the Persians and Romans – after Iman[1] of course – was the moral dissolution of those two great empires. The pure new blood, represented by the students of the Prophet's school, confronted a depraved, worn out blood of the two empires' soldiers. It was not unexpected that Iman could have overpowered Kufr[2], that strength could have defeated weakness, nor that solidarity could have conquered social instability. They also knew that we only lost our great glories when we opened our hearts, minds and homes to the corruption of those nations; their vices destroyed our vitality. Therefore, our defeat, at that time, was the defeat of morality rather than a defeat in the battlefield.

Indeed, our enemies drew plans that were to prevent Muslim women from performing an effective constructive role, so they would be drawn into circles of Fitna, under the deceptive guise of aluring terms, such as liberalism, renewal and progress. One famous colonialist said: "A glass (of wine) and a female singer do more

---

[1] Islamic faith.
[2] Disbelief: to reject Allah and refuse to believe that Muhammad is His Messenger.

damage, in the destruction of the nation of Muhammad, than a thousand canons. So sink it in the love of desires and materialism".

One leader of Freemasonry said: "We have to gain control of women, so whenever she stretches her hand to us, we will leave Haram (i.e. we will spread it in their society), and we will scatter their army, fighting for their religion".

It was reported in "The Protocols of the Zionist Rulers": "We have to work hard for the destruction of morality everywhere, to facilitate our control. Freud is one of us, and so he will continue to explain that sexual relations underlie all actions until nothing remains holy in the eyes of the youth, and their main concern would be to satisfy their sexual instincts; thereby, their morals would collapse".

It hurt them to see Muslim women generously providing the Ummah with active scholars and truthful Mujahideen; therefore, their main interest was to sterilize her, so as not to produce the likes of 'Umar bin Al-Khattab, Khalid bin Al-Walid, Salah Uddin Al-Ayyoubi (Saladin), 'Aisha bint Assiddik, Sumayyah bint Khubat, Asma', and Al-Khansa' to name but a few. The Muslim woman during the previous centuries remained secure and comfortable upon her throne, lifting the cradle with her right hand, and shaking the bases of Kufr with her left hand. So her enemies started their conspiracies against her, setting traps and hatching their plots to ambush her using all their means, until they achieved their goals in record time. Furthermore, they did not lift their hands away from our Ummah, nor remove their armies from our lands, until they were assured that they had left behind an army securing their aims and safeguarding their agreement; an army consisting of leaders of intellect, literature and "art", among the delusive elements called, wrongly, "the liberals and renovators". You see them disguised under their turbans, sometimes as faithful scholars, and sometimes revealing their true faces expressing their hatred towards those who enjoin the good and justice among people; even though, they themselves once claimed to be the protectors of the religion, and the callers to the faith.

The Main Case: The Qur'an and The Sultan

"Shari'a is a source, and the king is the guardian. So, that which has no source is destructible, and that which has no guardian is a lost thing",

Imam Abu Hamid Al-Ghazali.

Islam as a whole does not break up, and all the aspects of deviation from this Deen are but the outcome of the loss of "the Sultan"; 'Uthman bin 'Affan ﷺ once said: "People (Muslims) are restrained by the Sultan more than by the Qur'an"[1].

---

[1] Narrated by Yahya bin Sa'id, and transmitted by Rezin, it is among the known quotes of 'Uthman ﷺ.

Islam grants the Sultan mandatory powers to protect the Deen, and rule with it; he is entrusted with the lives of the nation, and the interests of the people. The enemies of Islam became aware of this great source among the sources of power of the nation, so they strived to destroy this firm bond in Islam. They achieved their goal when they launched their attack on the latest form of Khilafah (the Ottoman Caliphate), therefore, it fulfilled the saying of the Prophet ﷺ: "The ties of Islam will be lost one by one; whenever a tie is lost, people will grab hold of the one that follows it. The first one would the ruling by Islamic law, and the last one would be Salat"[1]. The fall of the Khilafah was the first descending step to degrade the Ummah and throw it into the lowest levels, which stripped it off its distinguished characteristics inherited through generations of dignity. The first generation of Islam armed with its honor and strength managed to conquer the oppressors, the Caesars (Roman emperors) and the Khosraus (kings of Persia)…

The return of Islamic rule and the Muslim Sultan has become the wish of every Muslim in the world; their hearts have united towards it, however, they have differed greatly on the method of achieving this long anticipated return, which Allah ﷻ Has promised: ❴**It is He Who has sent His Messenger with guidance and the religion of truth (Islam), to make it superior over all religions even though the polytheists hate it**❵[2]. Despite the divergent proposed methods used to attain

---

[1] Transmitted by Imam Ahmad, Ibn Hibban, and Al-Hakim, on the authority of Abu Umamah ☀.
[2] Surah At-Tawbah, Verse 33.

22

this goal, and the differences of their people, everyone is bound to agree that the first step is to reform ourselves, as one poet has said: "The shadow will not be straight if the stick is bent". Therefore, it has become our duty to rectify our understanding of Islam, of which we are striving to establish, by counteracting all the dominating intellectual invasions in many fields, and committing ourselves to this reformed understanding.

Among those dangerous areas, the situation of women… it is a serious case, which is not to be disregarded, until the realization of the aspired aim, by the will of Allah ﷻ. Indeed, the principle reason of its importance is that the establishment of the Islamic state and the revival of the Muslim Ummah depend on the situation of women in many aspects…

Women are the mothers of Mujahideen, daughters of Mujahideen, wives of Mujahideen, sisters of Mujahideen, so without "Muslim women" and "the Muslim home", the establishment of the "Islamic state" remains an out-of-reach goal. The return of Islamic rule would be achieved only at the hands of those who have the will to practice Islam within themselves and at home, and command themselves and their families, first, to the revelation of Allah ﷻ, in order to receive the victory from Allah ﷻ, when confronting the enemies of Allah; **❨Verily! Allah will not change the good condition of a people as long as they do not change their state of goodness❩**[1].

---

[1] Surah Ar-Ra'd, verse 11.

So, if we, Muslims, were unable, at some stage, to effectively practice the Revelation of Allah, with regards to the Hudud (Divine ordinance) etc, I (the author) still believe that we can, in many stages, and with the help of Allah ﷻ, rule according to the Revelation of Allah ﷻ in our homes, and we are still able to extract our understanding of Islam, in the case of woman, in particular, from the pure sources of Islam. Therefore, we should not stand confused, looking for the way out, while we have, in our hands, the inexhaustible help in the Book of Allah and the Sunnah of His Prophet ﷺ.

Between Compromising and Purity of Origin

Compromising and "imitation" are rejected as methods on the path to Islamic reform; in fact, the present day situation of women, justified, by some people having a defeated mentality, by using some Islamic texts, but this is a compromise of Islamic rules, which do not need any transformation in order for people to accept them. *Because Divine rules embody a hidden attraction, sensed by the hearts of all the believers who desire Allah as their Lord, Islam as their religion, and Muhammad ﷺ as the Prophet and Messenger.*

Muslim men and women's imitation of others is a sign of inner defeat, exemplified by this blind dependency, which has damaged their purity of origin and bereaved them of their "Islamic honor", it has also made them attach little importance to their Lord, and become careless of themselves.

"Woe to The Defeated From The Victorious"

How excellent the scholar Ibn Khaldoun (May Allah Have Mercy upon him) was; he dedicated a special chapter in his "Preface", titled: "The defeated person is often attracted towards imitating the victorious: in his anthem, dressing, faith, and all his traditions"; he explained that usually the one who imitates others is weak, deficient, defeated and ignorant, he also said:

"...You see the defeated imitates the victorious completely: in his dress, means of transport, and his choice of weapon, in all their forms. You witness this example in the way children always imitate their fathers, which is due to their belief in their fathers' perfection. The same example applies to two neighbouring nations, with one more powerful than the other, as it is the case of the present Andalusia with the Spanish nation; they identify themselves with their way of dressing, and many of their habits, even in having images on the walls of their factories and houses, such that a wise onlooker would consider it a sign of being under occupation; so the matter is with Allah 🕮".

Ibn Khaldoun was, indeed, right, for he had anticipated the occupation of Islamic Andalusia by the Spanish, and the expulsions of the Muslims, two centuries before it took place; he did not have any proof other than his witnessing of the Muslims' imitation of their enemies.

To have pride in Islam, honour its Divine ordinances, and exalt it above all opposing systems and methods, is the key to our return to Islam, and the return of Islam in our lives.

"Islam Rises High, and is Not to be Surpassed"[1]

Let us contemplate this story transmitted by Al-Hakim, on the authority of Ibn Shihab who said: "We set out to Syria (Shaam) with 'Umar bin Al-Khattab, and Abu 'Ubaidah bin Al-Jarrah was also with us. They reached a muddy place, 'Umar ؓ got down from his camel, took off his socks, put them on his shoulders, and began crossing the mud with his camel. Watching all these movements, Abu 'Ubaidah said to him that he would not wish the people of Syria to see 'Umar in that state. 'Umar ؓ replied, angrily: "If someone else said so, I would have made an exemplary punishment for the

---

[1] Part of a Hadith transmitted by Al-Bukhari without mentioning its authority; Al-Hafidh bin Hajar said: "and I found its chain related to the Prophet ﷺ in a Hadith other than the one of Ibn 'Abbas ؓ, it was transmitted by Addarakutni, and Muhammad bin Harun Arruyani in his Musnad, on the authority of 'A'id bin 'Amru Al-Mazani with a sound chain; he added at the beginning of the story the following event: that 'A'id bin 'Amru came on the day of Fath (of Makkah) in the company of Abu Sufyan bin Harb, so the Prophet's Companions said: This is Abu Sufyan and this is 'A'id bin 'Amru. The Prophet ﷺ said: This is 'A'id bin 'Amru and this is Abu Sufyan, Islam is more honoured than that, Islam rises and comes first"; from "Fath Al-Bari" (3/22) – the Prophet ﷺ wanted to teach them to mention the Muslim first.

Ummah of Muhammad ﷺ. We were the most disgraced people (nation), and Islam has Honoured us; so if we seek honor outside what Allah ﷻ has given us, He ﷻ will disgrace us". And in another narration: Abu 'Ubaidah said: "O Amir Al-Mu'minin! The soldiers of Syria might see you in this condition?" 'Umar ﷺ replied: "We are a nation honoured by Allah with Islam, so we will not seek honour outside it".

Rub'i bin 'Amer was sent by Sa'd ﷺ, before the battle of Al-Kadisiyah, as a messenger to Rustum, the leader of the Persian armies. Rustum was sitting on a golden bed with a most valuable crown on his head in a hall decorated with silky cushions and rags. Rub'i entered the palace riding his horse ho trod on the carpet; he dismounted and tied it to some of the pillows, then he moved forward, dressed with his body armor, helmet and weapon. The guards said to him: '(put down) your weapon!' He replied: 'I did not come to look for you, I am responding to your invitation; so I shall stay the way I am, or I will go back'. Rustum intervened and said: 'Let him in'. Rub'i walked using his spear as a support, which pierced most of the cushions. They said to him: 'Why did you (Muslims) come?' He replied: "Allah has sent us to remove and save whom He wills from the worship of people to worship of Allah ﷻ, from the narrow circle of this world to its wideness and its comfort, from the oppression of religions to the justice of Islam"[1].

---

[1] From the book "What the world has lost with the fall of the Muslims", p.11

"When some Christian student delegations visited some Islamic countries to receive knowledge, despite the disapproval of the church leader, the students' parents and the priests of their church endeavoured to set up psychological barriers in the minds of those students, to prevent them from being influenced by the Islamic thinking and the Muslim's way of life. The church was so concerned about those students that it issued a clerical statement which said: Those silly youths who start their speech in their mother tongue, and then finish their talk in Arabic language, to let us know that they studied in Muslim schools; if they do not stop, the church will issue statements against them to prohibit them... As for the Jews; their interpretation of the Talmud, and the instructions of their rabbis are enough to set up the psychological and materialistic barriers between them and the rest, but without those barriers – regardless of whether they are right or wrong – the Jews would have lost their identity, for centuries, within other nations, which would have led to their extinction)[1].

"Moshe Dayan" Advises...

During one of his outings, the Israeli defense minister met a Muslim youth in the street of an Arab village. He greeted him in his Jewish way, but the youth, who had

---

[1] "The Prohibition of Muslims to seek help from the disbelievers", p.11

28

strong Iman (faith), refused to shake his hand, and said to him: "You are the enemies of our nation, you occupy our land, and you deny us our freedom; but the day to get rid of you is surely coming with the Will of Allah, the prophecy of our Prophet ﷺ will certainly take place: 'You shall fight the Jews, while you are on the eastern side of the river, and they are on the western side of it'". The sly Dayan smiled and said: "It's true! A day will come for us to leave this land, and we also find the source of this prophecy in our books...but when?" He carried on: "When it rises among you people who are so proud of their heritage, respect their Deen, value their culture, but on the other hand, if it rises among us people, who reject their heritage and disrespect their history... then you will have a stand, and then the rule of Israel would end".

The Position of Women and The Responsibility of The Rulers

"When the earth will come to shake under people's feet, you will not find among them anyone who would define his position or his destiny, for everyone would be taken by surprise, and none would have the chance to ask the others, or even think of it.

The observer that would be able to register this general action would have to be outside the scene, in a place away from its influence.

It looks as though the mind, which created the story of Juha cutting the tree branch from the wrong position, intended to offer this picture... the image of unconsciousness that follows such an action: Juha stood on the same tree branch he was trying to cut from its stem, without paying attention to the inevitability of his eventual fall. So when a passer-by warned him of his destined fall, which subsequently took place, Juha stood up and ran after him to ask him: "You were aware of my fall before it took place, I will not let you go until you inform me when my end is due!"

This picture represents the reality of a Muslim woman today; in her frantic rush towards the unknown, of which she never asked herself about its aims nor its content... it is a world that no one can escape from its pressure except one who manages to distance himself from its influence, within a secure frame of free-thinking, taking the necessary measures for any unexpected events"[1].

What is painful, in this sad reality, is that women have consented to enable this state of weakness to develop; she has thrown herself headlong against the current, which caries her away, wherever it is heading, never even thinking of resisting it. Indeed, all her efforts have become directed behind that current, which is inevitably leading to her downfall. Contempt reached its peak when they made her belief that following their course would take her up to the highest level; however, she was not aware that, in reality, she had been used like a volley-ball thrown in every direction by the hands of the players...

---

[1] "Contemplative views woman and society", by Muhammad Al-Majdoub, p (7-8).

and still, if she should speak, she would boast that she was raised high, upon the shoulders of her admirers, to the highest level!

This new woman voiced her enmity towards her Deen, so some people would consider her shortcoming to be in her brain and her Deen, yet what excuse do men have, who exploited her defect, and persistently forced her to her detriment.

This discussion about women does not end, because she represents one half mankind; what we need to confirm is that anything we write regarding women, is derived from our concern, as Muslims, towards our sisters in Islam; our endeavour is to preserve and protect them, it is not out of "enmity" towards them. One cannot imagine that a straight man should become an enemy to a woman; does she not represent his mother, wife, sister or relative? So how could he be against these?

Furthermore, we should not be duped by the lies of those who preach the message: "friendship to woman", calling for her liberation, and leading her gatherings. Yet, in reality, they are her archenemy; they trade with her case, and benefit from her disintegration, deceiving their victims with delusive terms, which make weak souls submit to the illusions of "liberation".

"Search for The Jews"

Political concepts have been developed, in this wide world, to allow any person, with insight, to discover the Zionist hand[1] behind the disintegration of morality among many nations. So, why do we neglect the role played by this hidden hand in our social issues, in general, and the issue of woman in particular? Due to the Jewish tactical planning, the problem, in reality, has become reduced to suggestions imposed on our feelings by their specialised authorities. Their aim is to prevent us from guiding our intellectual behaviour according to the standards defined by our minds and observed by our conscience.

There is a hidden interest aimed at the situation of a Muslim woman, in certain intended circumstances, to

[1] A look at the book "Stop This Cancer", by Dr. Saif Uddine Al-Bustani who analysed, in it, the Jewish protocols and their efforts to deprave and corrupt a woman to "free her", shows the truth about this Zionist hand as behind the corruption of the Muslim women. The planning of the World Zionist state, which aims at taking control of the whole world, after establishing the " David State", agrees that among the methods to follow is the war on morals, and break up of the family system, using any means possible:
The vice movies are distributed in the world by Zionist firms, along with indecent fashions and obscene magazines which are all produced by Jewish publishing companies. Also, many so-called "hero artists", who spread their vice in different colours in Muslim lands are jews. Allah ﷻ said:❨**They ever strive to do mischief on earth, and Allah does not love those who do mischief**❩.

32

take away her self-confidence and her characteristics. Certainly, the aim behind it is most damaging; it is the demolition of all the spiritual barriers that have preserved in this nation so far, its feelings of dignity and freedom, which have encouraged people to strive and sacrifice in the path of Allah ﷻ. They also wish to uproot the links that connect us deeply in our history, to the glory of the Divine Revelation, the Revelation that made our nation the best nation to have emerged to people.

The situation of Muslim women was left to be thrown about by any tempest that came along; so it was not wise to keep it subdued by the hands of people who follow their desires; for there is no doubt, it is the duty of everyone: young, adult, ruler or subject... however, the implementation of rules remains the responsibility of the leaders, to whom Allah ﷻ has put, in their hands, the destiny of the state, and the interests of its people. We should not lie back and say: "The nation wants...", because the nation is unaware of the plot behind these social deviations, and as long as it remains in its heedlessness, it is difficult – if not impossible – for it to be conscious of its reality. However, we should say: "Islamic duty and the benefit of the nation compel responsible people to hold the current back before it reaches the waterfall; so where is the solution, if not in the Islamic legislation, which suggests that a woman should give up her mad race of blindly imitating the West. The legislation that says to the destructive elements among people of vice (arts): "Give up your dirty work, the life of earnest nations has no room for the foolishness of the impudent, and the prattles of the despicable", the legislation that says to women: "Refrain!

33

For you have planted all sorts of land mines in people's alleys, with your immorality. Observe the limits of decency, suggested by divine ordinance, as instructed by all the prophets; for if you do not do it at by your free will, you will do it against it".

America, the plantation of Jewish vice, was no more concerned about the morals than the Muslim nation[1]; and "Petain", born in Paris, the stronghold of immorality and vice, was no more conscious of morality than the nation of the Qur'an[2]. We have lost our distinguished personality, so all we could do was to imitate the West, whose superiority we admit. We, willingly, run after it, until we find ourselves going down faster than them. We welcome and practise the West's social mistakes, believing they are the best in human progress, ever created, and when one of their 'great' leaders reveals these mistakes, we turn away to ignore him!

Therefore, the reform of the under-developed nations relies, primarily, on their leaders, who possess the reins of reform. It is true what the ancient Arab wise men have said: "reforming the immorality of the subjects is better than reforming that of the guardian"... but the validity of

---

[1] A law was decreed in some American states suggesting that women's shoe heels do not exceed a specified measure, and police officers were supplied with a saw to cut off any excess!

[2] In France, Marshal Petain declared, immediately after their surrender to the Germans in the WWII: 'The secret of this disaster lays in our immorality', and issued a legislation to define the measure of the woman's clothing to prevent Fitna... Niriri, the dictator of Tanzania issued similar legislation, and the Iraqi police, in 1968, used to chase women whose clothes were above their knees, punish them by spraying their legs with blue paint!

this opinion is restricted to its circumstances; for the conscious nations are the ones which advise planning to their leaders, and from their political awareness their rulers, derive their trends. However, groups, which have not fulfilled their political maturity, and do not have any clear goals yet – especially if it were newly recovering from centuries of stumbling – usually accept reforms only through laws, so the call for welfare has to be preceded first by good examples; such as rulers and people around them, followed by supporting laws, which punish whoever deviates from the path of the group... One of the traditions of Al-Farooq ('Umar bin Al-Khattab ﷺ) was that whenever he wanted to bring something to public notice, he used to gather his family and say to them: "I will order people to do such and such, and they, surely, will be looking at you the way birds look at meat; so by Allah! if I discover any of you doing anything against this matter, I will double his punishment".

The Position of The Callers to Islam With Regards to The Case of Women

《But Allah tells you the Truth, and He shows the Right Way》[1]

The callers to Islam preach the return to the true face of Islam, and they believe that they are addressing one of two people:

Either a Kafir (disbeliever), so their main task is to call him to believe and affirm the truth of Monotheism and the Revelation; or a Mu'min (believer), and so their duty towards him is to provide the proof about the judgement of Allah 🕮 and His Messenger 🕮 from the Holy Book and the pure Sunnah, and then he has to say: "We hear and we obey". For, these people (the callers to Islam) do not judge with their own opinions, in the case of woman or in any other case where Allah 🕮 has set His judgement; their main raised motto is Allah's verse: **《It is not fitting for a Believer, man or woman, when a matter has been decided by Allah and His Messenger, to have any option about their decision》**, He 🕮 also said: **《The answer of the Believers, when summoned to Allah and His Messenger, so that He can judge between them, is to say: "We hear and we obey"》** and He 🕮 said: **《O you who Believe! Do not put yourselves forward before Allah and His Messenger》**.

---

[1] Surah Al-Ahzab, verse 4.

Therefore, you do not see them judging with their own opinions, but with the words of Allah, the All Wise and All Knower; they do not judge in the favour of men against the interests of women, or for the benefit of women against the interest of men, because Allah ﷻ tells the Truth and shows the Right Way. It is not in the interest of women – or of the whole society – to live in confrontation with men, the way that has occurred in Europe and America, to the extent that male organisations emerged demanding men's rights against the dominion of women. If woman takes this path chosen by the enemies of Islam, then she would not gain anything, instead she would lose everything; Allah ﷻ has created women for the same, main purpose that He has created men, He ﷻ said: **(I only created Jinn and mankind to worship Me)**, and He ﷻ made happiness conditional, with them both by fulfilling that purpose (worship Me), and misery when rejecting it; He ﷻ said: **(But whosoever turns away from My Message, his life will be a dark and narrow one, and on the Day of Judgement, We will gather him blind)**.

Worshipping Allah is The Highest Level of Freedom

Islam compels men and women to worship Allah alone (with no associates), submitting to His Religion, for this worship produces the highest level of freedom; indeed, by turning to Allah alone, man liberates himself from any authority; he stirs his heart, and bows his head to none but the Creator of the heavens and earth[1].

So, it is freedom in the form of worship; and mankind cannot be truly free unless it understands and performs this worship.

Freedom outside Islam is void and meaningless; rather it is a disgraceful form of slavery, even if it appears to be freedom.   The submission to the *taghuts* (from the leaders, presidents, methods, laws, and systems that are desired, in opposition to the Divine Legislation) is truly the worship of other than Allah, and what a worship!

They run away from the worship they were created for, and fall into the slavery of Kufr and Satan.

We Are Both Victims

The Islamic legislation is infallible, and free from any injustice: **❨Verily Allah does not wrong people in any way, rather it is people who wrong themselves❩**, and if the situation of Muslim women becomes bad, in some circumstances, then the main reason is not due to her observing of Islamic regulations – Allah forbid – it is rather, primarily, her deviation from Islam.

---

[1] See "Collected Fatwas" by Sheikh Al-Islam, Ibn Taymiyah (10/593,598).

The injustice befalling women in our society is exactly the same as that endured by men; its cause is not due to the Islam that we practise, it is rather due to our remoteness from Islam, the separation of Islam, the True Religion, from real life and its system of regulations.

We Do Not Justify The Mistakes

We do not justify what ever has occurred to women through injustice or bad conditions; there are people who demand too much from her, and are not compassionate towards her physical weakness; but there are the tough fathers, and the ignorant husbands who beat their daughters and wives carelessly; there are others who neglect woman completely, and abuse her rights. We do not ignore this, yet we also know that it is a sickness, among many, affecting our Ummah (its men, women, and children). We praise any attempt to reform the depraved, however, we do not accept repairing an error with another error; we do not want to move from exaggeration to negligence, and from a straying from the Right Path to any other path. May Allah bless Imam Malik, who said: "The last era of this Ummah may only recover if they adopt the good established at its beginning".

We, as well, are keen not to participate in this injustice and lay all the blame on oppressed, ignorant women... How many of those women were told that their access to and attendance in education – in its present Jahili state – and their employment, whatever kind in mixed social groups, is a legal duty, and that it is a right, which she should not neglect. Women were told that her staying at home was an imprisonment; a detention, which paralysed her great potential; and that her profession, nowadays, is to be found away from home. So many bad scholars turn many women astray with their fatwas; and so many women would have been sincere in observing the Islamic regulations, if it were not for the confusion of bad scholars, the grief of "progressive" fathers, and "modern" husbands. Indeed, many Muslim women who were obedient to Allah and His Messenger were subjected to misunderstanding and maltreatment from their fathers and husbands, and as a result, were forced to give in, may Allah ﷻ forgive them. The truth is that men (whether fathers and husbands) are the ones primarily addressed when Allah ﷻ said: **〈O you who believe! Save yourselves and your families from Fire, whose fuel is people and stones〉**[1], and the Prophet ﷺ said: "Everyone of you is a guardian and is responsible for his charge; the ruler is a guardian and is responsible for his subjects; a man is the guardian of his family and responsible for his charges; a woman is a guardian of her husband's house and responsible for her charges"[2].

---

[1] Surah Tahreem, verse 6.
[2] Transmitted by Imam Ahmed, Al-Bukhari and Muslim, on the authority of Ibn 'Umar ﷺ

The Legislation of Allah ﷻ is an Accomplished Fact

We do not deny that there is wide enough gap between our way of living and how it should be. But, those who use this fact to justify the participation of women in the field of employment are mistaken; that leaving their homes and mixing with men has become a reality and an established fact, hence we should be compelled to accept and follow the trend!

Nevertheless, we say to every Muslim woman who aspires to Allah and the Day of Judgment, knowing that she is responsible of herself, once she stands before Allah ﷻ: That which is called "the accomplished fact" will remain in our Islamic scale as a rejected falsehood to the Last Day, because the Patterns of Allah, on earth, never change. The Truth is one and never changes! It does not matter how long falsehood stays, it will always remain false, even if all people should adopt it; as for the Truth, it will eventually prevail; it is the law of Allah ﷻ, which does not change; it is the instinct that Allah ﷻ has endowed His creation with; for Allah has created everything and can guide anyone; ⟪**No change will you find in the practice of Allah**⟫.

41

A Woman is a Victim between Two Jahili Eras

《Have they not travelled through the land, and have they not hearts wherewith to understand and ears wherewith to hear? Verily, it is not the eyes that grow blind, but it is the hearts which are in the breasts that grow blind》[1].

"Things become clear when referring to their opposite"

In order to search for a way to understand the situation of the Muslim women in our time, where she has fallen victim to "the twentieth century Jahiliyah", we have to go back in time to the situation of women during the "first Jahiliyah" of the pre-Islamic Arab world, and even those of other nations, which disregarded guidance from Divine Revelation. Therefore, we should realise that there has been a universal oppression of women by denying them their human rights.

Therefore, we should look at the way Islam has liberated women, elevated their status, and honoured them in the Book (Qur'an) and the Sunnah; and we should read about the lives of the Muslim women and how they became believers and worshipers in Islam, striving with patience, and the way they set an example in Islam as mothers, daughters, wives or scholars...

- Then we should be able to perceive:

---

[1] Surah Al-Haj, verse 46.

- The false propaganda spread by the enemies of the Muslim women about how they see "the situation of women in Islam".

- The real disgrace that women were subjected to by Non-Muslims, and are still enduring now, in the modern Jahiliyah.

- And then we shall feel, along with our mothers, wives, and daughters, the great blessings of Islam; its unlimited grace, and its tribute to the Muslim women; we should, therefore, announce with all our faith: "O Muslim women, do not lose the blessings of Allah by being ungrateful to Him".

The Position of Women in Other Nations[1]

Certainly, the searcher for the position of women before Islam would not find what pleases him; he would find a universal denial of all her human rights:

---

[1] Extracts taken from: "Woman between Islamic Jurisprudence and the Law", by Dr. Al-Sibai' (13-22); "What about Women", by Dr. Noureddine Atar (13-16); "The Muslim woman" by Wahbi Ghawaji (25-27); "Woman and Her Position" by Hissin (11-17); "The Arab woman" by Abdullah Afif ; "Al-Hijab" by Al-Mawdudi.

Women in Ancient Greece

She was so despised and disgraced that she was regarded as the filth of Satan's act. She used to be bought and sold at markets, denied all her rights, such as the right of inheritance, and the right to benefit from her money. Their famous philosopher, Socrates has said: "The existence of woman is the greatest source of crisis and deterioration in the world; woman resembles a poisoned tree, whereby its surface is beautiful, but when birds eat from it, they die instantly".

History tells us how vice and depravity spread in the Greek society; it was considered a sign of freedom for a woman to be a prostitute, or have many lovers; they set up statues for the singers and the adulterers. They applied the colours of holiness to vice, and introduced it in their temples, where adultery became a means to get them closer to their gods. Other sources have said that woman had the right to marry more than one man.

Women in Roman Times

Their motto regarding woman was "Her chain and her yoke are not to be removed"[1]. People were not obliged to include their own offspring (male or female) in their family; the baby would be put near the father's feet; if he picked him up, then that was a sign that he accepted it as part of his family, if not it meant he had refused to accept it, and then the baby would be taken to the public square,

---

[1] "Women in the Qur'an", by Al-'Akkad, p.54.

44

or place worship, and if it was a male, people would take it, otherwise, the newly born baby would be left to die of hunger, thirst, the heat of the sun or (winter) coldness. The father could include any foreigner he wished in his family, or could exclude any of his own children by selling them in the market. There was a law whereby if the son was sold three times successively, he would then be released from the authority of his father; whereas, the daughter would remain under his authority as long as he remained alive. Among the astonishing stories transmitted by some sources was the suffering of women, in the Roman times, under their famous motto: "A woman has no soul"; they used to torture her by pouring hot oil over her body, tie her to posts, or even tie an innocent woman to a horse's tail and ride at a maximum speed dragging her on the ground until she would die[1].

Women in Ancient China

A Chinese man had the right to sell his wife like a maid, but if she should become a widow, the husband's family would own her as part of the inheritance left by the deceased. The Chinese man also had the right to bury his wife alive!

---

[1] "Woman in Islam" by Sakeenah Zaitun, p.11

45

Women under the Hammurabian Law (of Ancient Babylon)

Women were counted as part of someone's (owned) cattle; if someone killed the daughter of another man, then he had to surrender his own daughter, to either be killed or owned by the other man, in compensation.

Women in Ancient India

In the ancient Hindu legislation: "Even the wind, death, hell, poison, snakes or fire are less worse than a woman".

Dr. Mustafa Al-Sibai' said: "In the law of Manu, a woman did not have the right of independence from her father, husband, or son. If all of them died, then she had had to belong to a relative of her husband; she did not have the right to live after the death of her husband, she had to burn herself to death, with him, on the same funeral pyre. This habit continued until it was abrogated by the Hindu religious people in the seventeenth century. Woman used to be sacrificed to gain the pleasure of the "gods", and request rain or blessings from them. In some ancient Indian lands, a tree was to be nourished by a girl every year!"[1].

Gustav Le Pont stated that a woman in India "regarded her husband as a representative of the gods on earth; and the celibate or the widows were outcasts and considered

---

[1] "Woman between Islamic Jurisprudence and the Law" p.18

to be untouchables in the Hindu society, and were in the position of animals. If a widow should lose her husband while she was still young, then she had to remain unmarried all her life; she was not to be treated like a human being; her gaze was considered (a source of) a curse, for anything she had set her eyes upon, and her touch defiled everything. So, she was advised to throw herself on to her husband's funeral pyre, otherwise, she would have to suffer a disgrace more bitter than the punishment of fire itself)[1].

Women in Ancient Persia

"It was legal to marry a mother, sister, aunt, or niece. During her menstruation, a woman was to be exiled away from the city, and only a servant could approach her to serve her food. A Persian woman, generally, was under the absolute authority of man, who could either sentence her to death, or grant her the right to live"[2].

---

[1] "The Indian Civilizations", by Gustav Le Pont (644-646). It was the rule of Islam (during the time of King Ornik Zaib (May Allah Bless him), which put an end to that injustice inflicted on the Indian woman, until the occupation of the English and their oppression of the Indian people, especially its Muslim population.
[2] "The Rights of Women in Islam", by Muhammad Rashid Rida (27-28).

Women in Ancient Jewish Thinking

Some Jewish sects regarded women as servants; the father had the right to sell his daughter when she was young. She could only inherit from her father if he had no sons, and could only inherit property. As for any cash – even if there were tremendous sums – she would have no share in it.

If inheritance was transferred to the girl, because she had no brother, then she was not allowed to marry someone outside her own Israelite tribe, or take the inheritance outside it. The Jews considers women as a curse because Eve seduced Adam ﷺ; they do not socialize with her when she undergoes her menstruation. Some of them used to set up a special tent for a woman who was in her monthly period, offer her bread and water, and keep her there until she became clean.

Women in the Ancient Christian Nations

The first Christian priests were alarmed by the spread of vice and the collapse of morality in Roman society, so they considered women to be fully responsible, because they were active in society: mixing with men, and indulging in places of entertainment. They concluded that marriage was an unnecessary relationship that should be abandoned, and that celibate people were nearer to god than the married. St. Tertullian has said: "A woman is a passage for Satan to enter into the soul of a man, thus disgracing him".

St. Sustam has said: "She is an existing evil, a desired plague, a danger to the home and family, a coveted but destructive and disastrous element."

In the fifteenth century, some theologians gathered in a house meeting to discuss 'Whether women have real bodies or body with a doomed destructive spirit?', they concluded that she was devoid of a spirit, dangerous and beyond salvation, and there was no exception from among all of eve's daughters, apart from Mariam (Mary) صلى الله عليه, the mother of Isa (Jesus) عليه السلام.

In 586 C.E (i.e. at a time when the Prophet ﷺ was young), the French held a conference to discuss whether: Women were human beings or not? Whether she had a spirit or not? And if she had a spirit, was it a human or an animal one? And if it was a human spirit, was it on the same level as that of man or below it? Finally, they concluded that she was a human being, but was created to only serve man.

The distorted Christian religion as practiced in the Western world today sees woman as a source of sin, and considers her as one of the doors of Hell for men, for she entices him to commit sins, so she is a source of calamities happening to humanity overall.

During the reign of Henry VIII, the English parliament issued an order banning woman from reading the "New Testament" of (The Bible), because she was impure. Some sources have said that he had established a British Social Council, in 1500 C.E, especially to torture women.

French civil law had ruled, after the French Revolution, that minors included children, mentally ill people, and women. This law amended, in 1938, still places some restrictions on the activity of married women.

According to general English law, women were not considered as individuals or residents until, approximately, the mid-nineteenth century, therefore, they did not have any personal rights with regards to the money they earned or even the clothes they wore. In fact, the English Law, until 1805, authorized man to sell his wife at a specified price of six pence (half a shilling). In 1931, an Englishman sold his wife for five hundred pounds, and his lawyer, defending him, said: "English Law, in 1801, specified the price of a wife at six pence, with the condition that the deal should be done with the wife's consent". The court replied that the Law had been abrogated, in 1805, by a Law banning the selling of wives or giving them up to other people; and after the proceedings, the court sentenced the man who sold his wife to ten months in prison.

In the magazine "The Islamic Civilization", issue: year 2, page 1078, there was an article about an Italian who sold his wife to another man by installments; but when the man failed to pay the last installment, the husband killed him.

Muhammad Rashid Rida said: "Among the peculiarities transmitted by some parts of the British press these days[1]; the fact that there are still, in the English countryside, men who sell their wives at a very cheap price – like

---

[1] The book was published in 12 Rabi' Al-Awal 1351 A.H, i.e. the traits of the past were still existing some seventy years ago.

thirty shilling – and the newspapers have mentioned the names of some of them"[1].

That was a brief glance at the situation of women in the civilized age, the so-called the twentieth century civilization, in fact, it was not a civilization at all, but a world of depravity and imorality.

Women in Jahili[2] Arabia

> *"By Allah! Before Islam, we had no respect for women, until Allah has sent down His revelation, and set up their share"*

'Umar bin Al-Khattab ⌖.

Women did not have the right to any inheritance, and men used to say: "We only inherited by the one who wielded a sword to defend our clan". If a man died, his son would inherit from him, and if there were none, then any of the next of male kin (a father, brother, or uncle), then, finally his daughters and wives would be added to those of the inherited, and receive the same treatment.

---

[1] "Women's Rights in Islam", by Sheikh Muhammad Rashid Rida, and Dr. Noreddine commented saying: "And similarly, a friend of mine who has finished his studies in America recently said that some Americans exchange their wives for a specified period, then they receive them back, exactly the way a countryman hires his mule, or a urban man rents any of his goods!".
[2] The Pre-Islamic era.

51

A woman enjoyed no rights from her husband; divorce was not limited, nor was polygamy. If a man died, leaving a wife as well as children from another woman, then the eldest son had priority over the wife of his father; for he considered her as his legacy and part of his father's wealth; if he wanted to marry her, he had only to throw a cloth upon her, otherwise, she had the right to marry whomsoever she wanted.

Ibn 'Abbas ﷺ said: "If a man died, his son had the right to take his wife; if he wanted he could hold her until she paid back the dowry, or she would be kept until she died then he would take her money".

Marrying the wives of the fathers was a common practice in Jahiliyah, and a woman used to be held against her will, maltreated or sometimes totally ignored. And if a man wanted to have a noble son, he would take his wife to a noble man, such as a poet or knight of the tribe, and would leave her with him until it became clear that she fell pregnant from him, then he would receive her back at home!.

Ibn 'Abbas ﷺ has said: "They used to force their maids into prostitution, then take their money"; and Qatadah ﷺ has said: "In Jahiliyah, man could gamble with his wife and money, and he would stand sadly looking at his property in the hands of others; so, it used to create a lot of enmity and hatred among them"[1].

---

[1] Mentioned by Attabari when explaining the Verse ⟨Satan wants only to excite enmity and hatred between you with intoxicants and gambling, and hinder you from the remembrance of Allah and from Salat. So, will you not then abstain?⟩ Surah Al-Ma'idah, Verse 91.

The Arabs in the pre-Islamic era had many deranged types of marriages:

-   A group of men would cohabit with a woman, then if she gave birth, she was given the right to relate the child to whomsoever she wished from those men.

-   The husband would take his wife to one of the noble leaders, known for his courage and generosity, so she could have a child from him[1].

-   Public fornication practiced especially with the slaves.

-   It was common for men to have mistresses and intimate companions, and they used to consider it as vileness[2].

-   The Mut'ah marriage; a temporary marriage, which is banned by Shari'ah and considered illegal, while the Shi'ite Imamiyah sect has legalized it[3].

-   The exchange marriage: two men exchange their wives.

-   A marriage where two men marry the daughter or sister or any girl under their guardianship to each other without any dowry; and this type of marriage was conducted on the grounds that a

---

[1] And these two types still exist among some nations, like Tibet and others; with the Arabs it was temporary and restricted, as mentioned.
[2] Nowadays, this type is commonly and publicly practiced in Europe.
[3] It is spread now in the Western society and they call it: Marriage through experience.

woman was considered the property of man; he dealt with her in the same way as he would have done with his cattle or money.

- As for the upper class Arabs, such as the Quraish, their marriage was conducted as is practiced, in Islam, now; with an engagement, dowry and contract. This was approved by Islam after canceling all the unjust norms against women, like forcing them into an unwanted marriage, or banning them from it altogether, or taking their dowry money away from them.

Among The Pre-Islamic Habits in Divorce

"Some women used to divorce their husbands in Jahiliyah"[1].

"In those times, women did not need to announce their divorce; the sign of divorce for countrywomen was to change the direction of the door of their tents towards the west if it was initially towards the east, or towards the north if it was initially towards the south"[2].

Among The Pre-Islamic Habits of Mourning:

In Jahiliyah, if a woman lost her husband, the rest of women from her tribe would gather to mourn with her, bareheaded; crying, yelling and hitting their faces to

---

[1] "Al-Aghani", by Abu Al-Faraj (16/102).
[2] Ibid.

express their sadness of losing a dear person, and at times their mourning would last a year.

The 'iddah[1] period in Jahiliyah was a whole year during which women used to practice the worst types of mourning; a widow used to wear her worst clothes and live in the darkest room; she used to neglect herself and her purity, by not: applying perfumery, cleaning her body, clipping her nails or cutting her hair. She used to stay away from people, and after a year, she would appear with the worst appearance and scent, waiting for a passing dog, to throw droppings at it, in a manner showing the utmost contempt for the period she spent alone, and a total respect to her deceased husband!

Umm Salamah ⚬ mentioned that a husband of a lady died and her eyes became sore, so people mentioned of her story to the Prophet ⚬. They asked him whether it was permissible for her to use kohl as her eyes were at risk of infection. He said, "Previously, when one of you was bereaved of a husband she would stay in her dirty clothes in a bad, unhealthy house (for one year), and when a dog passed by, she would throw a pat of dung at it. No, (she should observe the prescribed period 'Iddah) for four months and ten days"[2].

And among the women's habits in Jahiliyah, was the way they used to show their compassion for each other, in mourning; they used to rush to a widow to support her, in

---

[1] Legally prescribed period of waiting during which a woman may not remarry, after being widowed or divorced.
[2] Transmitted by Al-Bukhari, Imam Ahmed, Muslim, Attirmidhi, Annasai, Ibn Majah, and Imam Malik, on the authority of Umm Salamah.

her wailing, by weeping aloud with her. This help would become a debt on her, which she should pay back.

The Burial of Girls Alive in Jahiliyah

Some Arabs used to see the birth of a girl, in their family, as a sign of humiliation which they could not bear; it made them feel weak out of disgrace, so they used to let her live neglected until she died, or bury her alive, denying her the right to live. If we assume that this hideous crime was practiced among the majority of Arabs, then we would not have observed the huge armies, which conquered many lands, and controlled many nations; for they were their sons and nephews! So, the truth is that burying girls alive was only common within the tribes of Rabi'ah, Kindah, Tamim, and Tai'. Some people buried their daughters alive for fear of poverty[1]. Some tribes believed that Angels were daughters of Allah, so they killed their daughters, saying: "We shall send them to join the daughters of Allah", Allah 🕮 The Most High, The Supreme is High above, and free from all their accusations.

---

[1] So Allah 🕮 replied to them: ❨And kill not your children for fear of poverty. We provide for them and for you. Surely the killing of them is a great sin❩ and ❨Kill not your children because of poverty, we provide sustenance for you and for them❩. Allah 🕮 expelled (in the first verse) their expected fear of poverty, and (in the second verse) their present fear.

Qatadah ﷺ has said: "The tribes of Mudar and Khuza'ah used to bury their girls alive; they feared they might be considered weak, and other tribes would attack them"[1].

"A Man would order his wife to bury, alive, a maid girl, and let another live; so she would call women and to dig a hole in the ground; as soon as they saw her coming, they would put her in the hole and level the earth on top"[2].

Some people used to bury alive the newly born girls alive in a harsher way; this atrocious act would be postponed if the father was away on a trip, so it would not take place until she had grown up and was aware of her fate. Sometimes, they would be dropped from a high mountain. It was reported that 'Umar ﷺ once said: "I remember two things in Jahiliyah, the first makes me cry, and the second makes me laugh; the sad one is: I once took a daughter of mine, to bury her alive, and while I was digging the hole for her, she shook the dust off my beard, not knowing my intentions, so when I remember that, I cry. And the other was that I used to venerate a date as a god, placing it by my head, to guard me at night whenever I slept, but if I felt hungry in the morning I would eat it. So whenever I remember that, I laugh at myself"[3].

Al-Qurtubi said, explaining the verse: **❨Indeed lost are those who have killed their children, out of folly, without knowledge, and have forbidden (to feed them)**

---

[1] "Al-Qurtubi" (10/117).
[2] "Ad-Dir Al-Manthur" by Assuyuti (8/48).
[3] "Adwa' Al-Bayan" (9/63).

that which Allah has provided for them, inventing a lie against Allah. They have indeed gone astray and were not guided[1]: It was reported that a man among the Companions of the Prophet ﷺ was looking very sad in his presence, so the Prophet ﷺ said to him: "Why are you feeling so sad?", he replied: "O Messenger of Allah! I have committed a sin in Jahiliyah, and I fear Allah ﷻ would not forgive me, now that I am Muslim". He ﷺ said: "Tell me about your sin". He said: "O Messenger of Allah! I was one of those who killed their daughters; when my girl was born, my wife appealed to me to let her live. I spared her, and she grew up to become one of the beautiful women of the village; so men approached me, asking to marry her. I was furious out of pride, as could not accept either both her being married or her living alone without a husband. So I said to my wife that I needed to visit some relatives with my daughter; she was so pleased, she dressed her with her best clothes, and obliged me not to betray her. But, I took her to the top of a pit, and looked in it. Then she sensed that I was going to throw her in so she started crying, saying: O father! What do you want to do to me? Do not betray the trust of my mother. So I pitied her, but whenever I looked at the pit, I felt the urge to throw her in; an urge from Satan; so I grabbed her and pushed her into the pit. She started calling out: O Father! Why are you killing me? I stayed there until she stopped crying, then returned". The Prophet ﷺ and his Companions all had tears in their eyes. Then, he ﷺ said: "If I was ordered to punish people for what they did in Jahiliyah, I would have punished you"

---

[1] Al-An'am, verse 140.

i.e. the Prophet ﷺ meant that being in Islam removes the links with every Muslim's past sins.

Addarami reported in his Musnad: "A man came to the Prophet ﷺ and said: O Messenger of Allah! We were people of Jahiliyah; worshiping idols, and killing our children; I once had a daughter, whom I took to a pit that belonged to some other people, then threw her in it. Her last words were: 'O father! O father!' The Prophet ﷺ cried until tears dripped from his eyes. A man in the audience said to him: 'You have saddened the Messenger of Allah', but the Prophet ﷺ interrupted him, saying: 'Stop (let him speak), for he talks about his worries', then he ﷺ said to the man: 'Repeat your story to me'. He related his story again, and the Prophet ﷺ wept until tears dripped on his beard, and said: 'Allah ﷻ has forgiven what Muslims have done in Jahiliyah, so carry on doing good deeds'[1].

Abderrazak reported that 'Umar bin Al-Khattab said, referring to the Verse: **⟨And when the female (infant) buried alive (as the pagan Arabs used to do) shall be questioned, for what sin she was killed⟩**[2]: "Qais bin 'Asim came to the Prophet ﷺ, and said: 'O Messenger of Allah, I have buried my daughters alive in Jahiliyah'. So the Prophet ﷺ said: 'Free a slave for each one of them'. He said: 'O Messenger of Allah! I own camels'; so the Prophet ﷺ said: 'Then slaughter a camel for each one of them'".

---

[1] Transmitted by Addarami in the introduction of his Musnad, Chapter: The Jahiliyah life of the people before the Mission of the Prophet ﷺ.
[2] Attakweer, verses 8-9.

In the Glorious Qur'an, Allah has condemned this abominable act, and the way that newly born females were treated by the pagan Arabs, when He ﷻ said:

《And so to many of the pagans, their so-called partners, have made fair-seeming the killing of their children, in order to lead them to their own destruction and cause confusion in their religion. And if Allah had willed they would not have done so. So leave them alone with their fabrications.》[1]

《And according to their pretending, they say that such and such cattle and crops are forbidden, and none should eat of them except those whom we allow》[2], i.e. it is only eaten by men (and not women); and it was said: "The servants of the idols." Then Allah ﷻ shows that it was their own judgment, by saying: **《their pretending》 《And they say there are cattle forbidden to be used for burden or any other work, and cattle on which (at slaughtering) the Name of Allah is not pronounced; lying against Him (Allah). He will recompense them for what they fabricate. And they say: "What is in the bellies of such and such cattle..."》**[3]. Assuyuti[4] said: ibn Hibban transmitted, on the authority of ibn 'Abbas ﷺ, who said: "They used to ban their females from drinking "Milk", and only allow their males to have it; and if the sheep gave birth to a male, they would slaughter it and provide it as a meal for males only, and if it was a female, they would leave it.

---

[1] Al-An'am, verse 137.
[2] Al-An'am, verse 138.
[3] Al-An'am, verse 138-139.
[4] "Ad-Darr Al-Manthur" (3/48).

But if it were dead on birth, they both (males and females) would share it."

Al-Qurtubi said: "Allah ﷻ has informed us of their loss and doomed destiny for killing their children, and banning al-Baheerah and others following their own rational judgment…"[1].   Qatadah said: "This is the practice of the people of Jahiliyah: The man would kill his daughter for fear of poverty, but would feel his dog"[2]. Ibn 'Abbas ﷺ said: "If you are interested to know more about the ignorance of the pagan Arabs, then read the verses, after verse 130, of Surat Al-An'am".

Allah ﷻ said: ❨**And they assign daughters unto Allah! – Glorified (and Exalted) be He above all that they associate with Him! – And unto themselves what they desire; and when the news of the birth of a female child is brought to any of them, his face becomes dark, and he is filled with inward grief! He hides himself from the people because of the evil of that whereof he has been informed. Shall he keep her with dishonour or bury her in the earth? Certainly, evil is their decision**❩[3].

The tribes of Khuza'ah and Kinanah used to say: "The Angels are the daughters of Allah" as Allah ﷻ has started in the above verse, even though, they assigned females to Allah ﷻ, they disapproved of them for themselves, and they felt both sad and angry if they were informed that their newly born baby was a female. They despised their

---

[1] "Al-Qurtubi" (7/96).
[2] "Ad-Darr Al-Manthur" (3/48).
[3] An-Nahl, verse 58-59.

61

wives, for giving birth to females, and they avoided meeting their friends for fear of being seen in a sad state and so they felt disgraced.

The Light of Islam Shines Upon Women

(The light of Islam shines; it is a new opening for the destiny of Arab women, revealing a shining ray, a distant hope of a new way of life.

The foundations of Islam have been firmly established, and its effects are far reaching. Woman may taste and enjoy the bond of faith; she may also acquire the knowledge. She was duly granted rights that no other nation, at any time, had ever legislated for her. She carefully (and freely) studied the way of perfection, exposing the weaknesses of those before her, until no other woman in the world could have equaled her sublime position in life.

These were the woman that Islam produced, and they, in turn, raised others with it. The effect was to produce great men, and the establishment of its social system. These events were like a bubbling stream in a garden of flowers"[1].

---

[1] "The Arab Woman"(2/14).

Islam's Honouring of Women

Islam never considered women to be inferior, as perceived by other nations; it, however, reaffirmed the truth, removing any disgrace. Women, in Islam, are partners to men; she has her own rights, as well as some duties that conform to her constitution and nature. As for man, he has his responsibilities according to his specifications among which are: the honour of manhood and virility, the hardness of his skin, the power of his hand, which qualify him to be her governor; indeed, he is her guardian, who protects her with his strength, defends her with his life, and provides for her from his earnings. This is what Allah ﷻ has summarized in this verse:

《Women possess rights similar to those held over them, to be honoured with fairness; but men have a degree over them》[1].

That is the degree of care and protection; it is not to be extended to oppression and rejection of the Truth.

As Allah ﷻ has drawn a parallel between them in the affairs of life; He ﷻ made equaled in their level of humanity, friendship, religious commandments, repentance, accumulation of rewards, and potential elevation to the highest levels of Paradise.

---

[1] Surat Al-Baqarah, verse 228.

Equality in Humanity

Women and men are equal in humanity, Allah ﷻ has said: **❰Mankind! We created you from a male and a female, and made you into peoples and tribes, so that you might come to know each other. The noblest among you in Allah's sight is the righteous one. Allah is All-Knowing, All-Aware❱**[1], And she was created from man; as Allah ﷻ said: **❰O mankind! Be dutiful to your Lord who created you from a single person (Adam), and from him (Adam), He created his wife (Eve), and then disseminated many men and women from the two of them❱**[2].

He ﷻ created women as a blessing that men should thank God for, He ﷻ said: ❰Among His Signs is that He created spouses for you of your own kind, so that you might find tranquility in them. And He has placed affection and compassion between you❱[3], and He ﷻ said: ❰It is He who created you from a single self, and made from him his spouse so that he might find his repose in her❱[4]; and ❰Allah has given you wives from among yourselves, and given you children and grandchildren from your wives❱[5]. The Prophet ﷺ has said: "Women are partners to men"[6].

---

[1] Al-Hijurat, verse 13.
[2] An-Nisa', verse 1.
[3] Ar-Rum, verse 21.
[4] Al-A'raf, verse 189.
[5] An-Nahl, verse 72.
[6] Transmitted by Imam Ahmed, Attirmidhi, Abu Dawud, on the authority of Aishah ﵂.

Equality in Most Religious Commandments

The faith of women is equivalent to that of men's. Allah ﷻ said:

《O you who believe! When believing women come to you as emigrants, examine them, Allah knows best as to their faith, then if you know them for true believers, send them not back to the disbelievers》[1].

And He ﷻ said:

《And those who abuse believing men and women, undeservedly, bear on themselves the crime of slander and plain sin》[2].

He ﷻ also said:

《Verily those who put into trial the believing men and believing women (by torturing them and burning them), and they do not turn in repentance, (to Allah), will have the torment of Hell, and they will have the punishment of the burning Fire》[3].

Allah ﷻ ordered His Prophet to seek His forgiveness for all believing men and believing women; as He ﷻ said:

《So know that there is no god except Allah and ask forgiveness for your wrongdoing, and for the

---

[1] Al-Mumtahinah, verse 10.
[2] Al-Ahzab, verse 58.
[3] Al-Buruj, verse 10.

believing men and believing women, Allah knows both your activity and your repose》[1].

The Prophet ﷺ said: "Whoever asks Allah ﷻ for His forgiveness for the believing men and believing women, Allah records, with each one of them, a good deed (for him)".

What is agreed upon, and considered essential in Islam, is that women have the same obligations, with regards to the fundamentals of Islam, as men; however, during her period of menstruation, she is not required to do Salat, and she is not obliged to settle it after, because they are too many. In Ramadan, woman does not fast when she has menstruation, but does have to settle the days she did not fast in Ramadan, because they are few. As for Hajj, it is valid for her in any situation, but she has to be pure (not menstruating) to perform the circumambulation of the Ka'ba.

Equality in the Level of Rewards in The Hereafter

Allah ﷻ said: **《Whoever works righteousness, whether male or female, while he (or she) is a true believer, verily to him We will give a good life, and We shall pay them certainly a reward in proportion to the best**

---

[1] Muhammad, verse 19.

of what they used to do (i.e. Paradise in the Hereafter)》[1].

Allah ﷻ said: 《Whosoever does an evil deed, will not be requited except the like thereof, and whosoever does a righteous deed, whether male or female and is a true believer (in the Oneness of Allah), such will enter Paradise, where they will be provided therein (with all things in abundance) without limit》[2].

Allah ﷻ said: 《And whoever does righteous deeds, male or female, and is a true believer in the Oneness of Allah, such will enter Paradise and not the least injustice, not even the size of a tiny speck, will be done to them》[3].

Allah ﷻ said, about men of understanding who remember Him (always, and in prayers), and think deeply about the creation of the heavens and the earth: 《So their Lord accepted of them their supplication and answered them, "Never will I allow to be lost the work of any work of you, be he male or female. You are members of one another"》[4].

One should reflect on how the Qur'an confirms this principle, as Allah ﷻ has said: 《Verily, the Muslims (who submit to Allah in Islam), men and women, the believers, men and women (who believe in Islamic

---

[1] An-Nahl, verse 97.
[2] Ghafir, verse 40.
[3] An-Nisa', verse 124.
[4] Al-Imran, verse 195.

Monotheism), the men and the women who are obedient to Allah, the men and women who are truthful (in their speeches and deeds), the men and the women who are patient (in performing all the duties which Allah has ordered and in abstaining from all that Allah has forbidden), the men and the women who are humble (before their Lord - Allah), the men and the women who give Sadaqat (i.e. Zakat, and alms, etc), the men and the women who fast, the men and the women who guard their chastity, and the men and the women who remember Allah much (with their hearts and tongues); Allah has prepared for them forgiveness and a real reward (i.e. Paradise)》[1]. So Allah ﷻ has equalized the importance of a husband or wife, son or daughter, male or female servant using appropriate attributes. Our ancestors, May Allah be pleased with them, had indeed adopted this path; one can learn how their children, women and servants used to, generally, possess all these characteristics.

Allah ﷻ has said: 《Allah has promised the believers, men and women, Gardens, under which rivers flow, to dwell therein forever, and beautiful mansions in Gardens of Paradise. But the greatest bliss is the Good Pleasure of Allah. That is the supreme success》[2].

Allah ﷻ said: 《That He may admit the believing men and the believing women to Gardens under which rivers flow (i.e. Paradise), to abide therein forever,

---

[1] Al-Ahzab, verse 35.
[2] Tawbah, verse 72.

and to expiate from them their sins, and that, in the Sight of Allah, is a supreme success⟩[1].

Allah ﷻ said: ⟨On the Day you shall see the believing men and the believing women – their light running forward before them by their right hands. Glad tidings for you this Day! Gardens under which rivers flow (Paradise), to dwell therein forever! Truly, this is the great success!⟩[2].

The Prophet ﷺ said: "If a woman performs her five daily Salats, fasts Ramadan, Guards her chastity (from illegal sexual acts), obeys her husband (in the obedience to Allah); then she will be told: 'Enter Paradise from any of its doors you wish'"[3].

Umm Salamah ؆ said: The Prophet ﷺ said: "Any woman who dies when her husband is pleased with her will enter Paradise"[4].

'Ubaadah bin Assamit ؆ said that, one day, the Prophet ﷺ visited Abdullah bin Rawahah who was ill. When he moved away from his bed, he ﷺ said: "Do you know who are the martyrs of my Ummah?" They said: "The Muslim who is killed is a martyr". He ﷺ said: then the

---

[1] Al-Fath, verse 5.
[2] Al-Hadid, verse 12.
[3] Transmitted by Ibn Hibban, Al-barraz, Imam Ahmad, and Attabarani, and it was authenticated by Sheikh Al-Albani ▯▯▯▯ ▯▯▯▯
[4] Transmitted by Attirmidhi who said: "A sound and strange Hadith". Also transmitted by Ibn Majah and Al-Hakim.

martyrs of my Ummah would be few! The Muslim who is killed is a martyr, the Muslims who die of any plague are martyrs, and the woman who died while pregnant is a martyr, for her baby drags her along to Paradise with its umbilical cord".

Among the proofs confirming the fact that women and men are equal, in gaining requital and reward is the following Hadith:

Asma' bint Yazid bin As-Sakan ﷺ came to the Prophet ﷺ and said: "I am representing a group of Muslim women; they all have my opinion: 'Allah ﷺ has sent you to both men and women; we have believed in you and followed you. We women are restricted and kept in seclusion in our homes, while men are given preference for the Jumu'ah Salat, their attendance at funerals and for Jihad; if they set out for Jihad, we preserve and protect their wealth, and bring up their children. So, do we have a share in their reward, O Messenger of Allah?"

The Prophet ﷺ turned his face to his Companions ﷺ and said: "Have you ever heard a woman asking a better question about her Deen than this one?" they said: "No, O Messenger of Allah". The Prophet ﷺ said to her: "You may go, O Asma', and inform the rest of the women that the good matrimonial behaviour, of any of you, to her husband; seeking his pleasure and gratification and following his consent, does in fact equal all the things you have mentioned concerning men". So Asma' went home fully content, saying *la ilaha ila Allah,* rejoicing with these glad tidings of the Messenger of Allah[1].

Equality in Friendship and Support

Allah ﷻ said: ❨The believing men and believing women are friends of one another. They command what is right and forbid what is wrong, and establish Salat and pay Zakat, and obey Allah and His Messenger. They are the people on whom Allah will have Mercy. Allah is Almighty, All-Wise❩[2]

Equality Among Believing Women

Islam has removed many types of discrimination that previously existed among women, as it has done for those that existed among men. So people's heads have been lowered, and their souls have been made equal. Nothing, not even her old lineage that she used to be honored with, can put her ahead of other women, before Allah ﷻ, but only her good deeds that she strives for would distinguish her from others.

---

[1] Transmitted by Ibn Abd Al-Barr in his "Al-Isti'ab" (4/233), and it was reported by Muslim as well.
[2] At-Tawbah, verse 72.

71

Allah ﷻ has legislated the notion of brotherhood, when He ﷻ said: ❴**The believers are brothers**❵[1]. Therefore, there is no distinction between a Muslim woman and a Muslim man, or between a Muslim man and the Muslim woman, except when comparing one possessing sublime morals with one having vile ones; for Allah ﷻ has expressed His Wisdom when He ﷻ said: ❴**Corrupt women are for corrupt men, and corrupt men are for corrupt women. Good women are for good men and good men are for good women**❵[2]. The Prophet ﷺ had issued the principle of equality when he ﷺ said: "A Muslim is a brother of another Muslim"[3], and he ﷺ said: "All types of lineage and relationships by marriage will be cut off on the Day of Resurrection, except my lineage and my in-laws' relationship"[4], and the following Hadith is also a strong proof of this principle: It is known as the Hadith of Fatimah bint Al-Aswad Al-Makhzumiyah – a woman from a noble family of the Quraish – who once committed theft, and the evidence was against her, so the Islamic legal punishment was to be applied to her. The

---

[1] Al-Hujurat, verse 10.

[2] An-Nur, verse 26.

[3] Transmitted by Muslim, on the authority of Abu Hurairah ﷺ. Abu Dawud transmitted it, on the authority of Handhalah ﷺ. As for Attirmidhi, he transmitted it on the authority of Abu Hurairah ﷺ with the rest of the Hadith: "…he neither betrays him, nor lies to him, nor humiliates him, nor looks down upon him. Piety is here – and he ﷺ pointed to his chest (heart). It is serious (evil) for a Muslim that he should look down upon his brother Muslim. All things of a Muslim are inviolable for his brother in faith; his blood, his faith, and his honour".

[4] Transmitted by Ibn 'Asakir, on the authority of Ibn 'Umar ﷺ, and it was authenticated by Sheikh Al-Albani in "Sahih Al-Jami' Assaghir" (4/182).

people of the Quraish were worried and they asked: "Who can intercede with the Prophet for her?" So nobody dared to speak to him ﷺ but Usamah, his most beloved. The face of the Prophet ﷺ showed great disappointment, and he ﷺ said: "People before you have perished; if a reputable man among them committed a theft, they used to forgive him, but if a poor man committed a theft, they used to cut his hands. But I would even cut the hands of Fatimah (i.e. the daughter of the Prophet) if she committed a theft". He ﷺ ordered for the punishment to take place on that woman, and 'Aishah ﷺ said: "She excelled in her repentance afterwards and even got married. She used to visit us and I would take all her requests and queries to the Prophet ﷺ"[1].

Allah ﷺ censured women scoffing and ridiculing one another, when He ﷺ said: ﴿O you who believe! Let not a group scoff at another group, it may be that the latter is better than the former; nor let (some) women scoff at other women, it may that the latter is better than the former﴾[2]. It was said that this verse was revealed when Safiyah, daughter of Huyay bin Akhtab came to the Prophet ﷺ and said: "Women are making fun of me; they say: "O Jewish woman, daughter of Jewish parents". The Prophet ﷺ said: "Why not say to them: "My father is Harun, my uncle is Musa (Moses), and my husband is Muhammad", so the verse was revealed in Surat Al-Hujurat. The warning is general in meaning, not particular to the reason of its revelation.

---

[1] Transmitted by Al-Bukhari, Muslim, Attirmidhi, Abu Dawud, and Annasai, on the authority of 'Aishah ﷺ.
[2] Al-Hujurat, verse 11.

Some Aspects of Islam's Mercy on Women

"Can you imagine the state a servant girl who was looking after a herd (of a sheep or goats) in a field, when a wolf came and ate one, then her master did not hesitate to beat? Would that be a strange story to believe for people living so far away from that time and place? But, this had actually happened at the time of the Prophet ﷺ. The man (the girl's master) went to the Prophet ﷺ, informing him of what he had done to his servant girl. The Prophet ﷺ was so furious that his face turned red, and his Companions were too frightened to address him ﷺ. The man stood motionless, and the Prophet ﷺ said: "What could the girl do against the wolf? What could the girl do against the wolf!" he ﷺ kept repeating it, then he ﷺ added: "Your servants are your brothers (and sisters), and Allah has given you guardianship over them". The man could do nothing to reprieve himself, but to free the girl servant"[1].

The Messenger of Allah ﷺ had inherited a servant woman from his father; she had a slight speech difficulty that she could hardly be recognized as Umm Ayman, so the Prophet ﷺ used to call her mother, and whenever he ﷺ looked at her, he would say: "She is all that is left of my family"[2].

---

[1] "The Arab Woman", by Abdullah 'Afifi (2/21).
[2] "Atabakat Al-Kubra" by Ibn Sa'd (7/162).

74

The Prophet ﷺ used to get deeply hurt when he heard any man insult another by mentioning his mother (in the insult); Al-Ma'rur bin Suwaid once reported: "I saw Abu Dhar Al-Ghafari wearing a cloak, and his slave, too, was also wearing a cloak. We asked him about that (i.e. how both were wearing similar cloaks). He replied, 'Once I abused a man and he complained of me to the Prophet. The Prophet asked me, "Did you abuse him by slighting his mother?" He added, "Your slaves are your brethren upon whom Allah has given you authority. So, if one has one's brethren under one's control, one should feed them with the like of what one eats, and clothe them with the like of what one wears. You should not overburden them with what they cannot bear, and if you do so, help them (in their hard job).'" This comprehensive brotherhood was what made 'Umar bin Al-Khattab ؓ marry his favorite son, 'Asim, to the daughter of a woman who used to sell milk on the road, whereas if he had wanted, he could have married him to the most honored woman in the world.

Some of The Prophet's Kindness and Mercy to Women

'Umar bin Al-Khattab ؓ requested to see the Prophet ﷺ, so the women in his gathering immediately put their Hijab on. When 'Umar ؓ entered, the Prophet ﷺ smiled, so 'Umar ؓ said: "What makes you laugh, O Messenger of Allah?", he ﷺ replied: "The woman saw you coming, so they put on their Hijab". 'Umar ؓ turned to them and said: "O enemies of themselves! You fear me, but you do not fear the Prophet ﷺ?", they replied: "You are tougher and rougher than the Messenger of Allahﷺ"[1].

Among the aspects of his kindness to women is the event of when some women came to pledge allegiance to him ﷺ, that they would implement the commandments of Allah ﷻ and would abstain from His prohibitions; he ﷺ said: "…to your ability". So the women replied: "Allah and His Messenger are even more merciful to us than ourselves"[2].

The Prohibition of Killing Women in Wars

Yahya related to me from Malik from Ibn Shihab that a son of Ka'b bin Malik (Malik believed that bin Shihab said it was Abd ar-Rahman bin Ka'b) said, "The Messenger of Allah ﷺ, forbade those who fought ibn Abi Huqayq (a treacherous Jew from Madinah) to kill women and children. He said that one of the men fighting had said, "The wife of ibn Abi Huqayq began screaming and I repeatedly raised my sword against her. Then I remembered the prohibition of the Messenger of Allah ﷺ, so I stopped. Had it not been for that, we would have

---

[1] Transmitted by Al-Bukhari.
[2] "Atabakat Al-Kubra" (7/4-6).

76

been rid of her"[1]. Therefore, it is forbidden to kill women, children and the old people, except if they participate in fighting, then they would be killed in defense only. Ibn 'Umar ﷺ said: "A woman was found killed in one of the battles of the Prophet ﷺ, so he ﷺ prohibited the killing of women and children"[2].

His kindness to Ashaima' Bint Al-Harith bin Abd Al-'Uza bin Rafa'ah (his foster sister)

Ibn Sa'd said: "Ashaima' and her mother used to nurse the Prophet ﷺ as a child; and Abu 'Umar said: 'The army of the Prophet ﷺ invaded the tribe of Hawazin, and they took her (Ashaima') as captive. She said to them: "I am the sister of your companion (Muhammad)", and when they brought her, she said: "O Muhammad! I am your sister" and she informed him of a mark he ﷺ has on his body, and he recognized her; so he ﷺ welcomed her, he laid down his cloak, and seated her. He ﷺ had tears in his blessed eyes, so he said to her: If you wish to return to your people, I will take you there, and if you prefer to stay, you will be much honoured and loved". She replied: "I'd rather go back, so she embraced Islam, and the Prophet ﷺ gave her cattle, three slaves and a maid"[3].

---

[1] Transmitted by Malik and Al-Isma'ili.
[2] Transamitted by Al-Bukhari and Muslim.
[3] "Attabakat" by Ibn Sa'd (8/250).

The Conduct Towards The Menstruating Woman as Detailed in The Sunnah

'Aishah ؎ said: "I would drink when I was menstruating, then I would hand it (the vessel) to the Prophet ؎ and he would put his mouth where mine had been, and drink"[1].

Abdullah ibn Sa'd Al-Ansari ؎ said: "I asked the Prophet ؎ about whether or not I would dine with my wife while she is menstruating". He replied: 'Dine with her'"[2].

'Aishah ؎ said: "The Messenger of Allah ؎ said to me: 'Get me the mat from the mosque'. I said: 'I am menstruating'. Upon this he ؎ remarked: 'Your menstruation is not from your hand'"[3].

And she ؎ also said: "The Prophet ؎ used to lean on my thighs (while I was menstruating), while he recited the Qur'an"[4].

The Dignity of Muslim Women

Islam draws a parallel between men and women in general; it acknowledges their tenderness, and sensitivity. She is the subject of man's honour and she plays a big

---

[1] Transmitted by Muslim, Abu Dawud and Annassa'i.
[2] Transmitted by Attirmidhi.
[3] Transmitted by Muslim.
[4] Transmitted Al-Bukhari, Muslim, Abu Dawud and Annassa'i.

78

part with regards to his dignity; therefore, Islam has sanctified her, which is not the case of her counterpart man.

The dignity of woman in Islam encompasses her personality and her life; she deserves to be cared for and to be safe from defamatory talk. Women used to grant sanctuary to the persecuted, and free the distressed by their respect and honour, of which they have reached the highest degree.

Umm Hani', daughter of Abu Talib, once granted sanctuary to two men, among her relatives, who had been sentenced to death; she said: "When the Prophet ﷺ conquered Makkah, two men from among my relatives of Banu Makhzum came running to me, seeking my protection, then my brother Ali bin Abu Talib entered and said: 'By Allah, I will kill them!' So I locked them inside and went to see the Prophet ﷺ who greeted me: 'Welcome to you Umm Hani'. What is the reason of your visit?' So I informed him about the state of the two men and Ali; he ﷺ said: 'We shelter those whom you have sheltered, and we (also) safeguard those whom you safeguard; so (now) Ali will not kill them'.[1]

When the Muslims captured Abu Al-'As bin Arrabi', and took his wealth as bounty – Abu Al-'As was the husband of Zainab, daughter of the Messenger of Allah, before Islam separated them – he sought protection from Zainab ﷺ who promised him safety. She waited until the Prophet ﷺ had performed Salat Al-Fajr (Dawn Salat) with the Companions, then she stood by the door of the

---

[1] Transmitted by Al-Bukhari.

mosque, and shouted: "I have granted sanctuary to Abu Al-'As bin Arrabi'". The Prophet ﷺ said: "Have you heard what I heard?" they said: "Yes", so he ﷺ said: "By Whom my life is between His Hands! I did not know anything of this until now (until I heard what you have just heard), for the believers have (authority and) power over the rest of the people; those below them have to seek their protection. Thus, we shall give shelter to whom Zainab has given shelter". And when the Prophet ﷺ left for his house, Zainab ﷺ went to see him and asked him if he ﷺ could return to Abu Al-'As everything that was taken away from him, to which he ﷺ obliged and agreed[1].

As for the sanctity of their lives and the safeguarding of their reputation, no other legislation has put so much emphasis on them as Islam; it suffices to say that Allah ﷻ has promised a severe punishment, as mentioned in the Qur'an, for those who slander the honour of the Muslim women believers, even more than He ﷻ has prepared for criminals; He ﷻ said: ﴾**But those who make accusations against chaste women, and then do not produce four witnesses: flog them with eighty slashes and never again accept them as witnesses, such people are deviators (liars, disobedient to Allah)**﴿ An-Nur: 4.

He ﷻ decreed eighty slashes for slander, and He ﷻ enforced this punishment with an even more severe one: that of labeling him eternally as a liar, thus rejecting his

---

[1] Abu Al-'As returned later to Makkah, he gave everyone their rights, and headed towards Al-Madinah as a Muslim; he was greeted by the Messenger of Allah ﷺ who returned Zainab to him. See "Al-Isabah" (7/247).

testimony forever, and finally He ﷺ branded him with a term that is worse even that of the other three: that of Fisq (sinfulness and rebelliousness).

That is not the only punishment for those sinners and criminals; He ﷺ reverted to their matter with more frightening punishment: ❨Those who accuse women who are chaste, but who are careless and yet are good believers, are cursed both in this life and the in the Hereafter, and they will have a terrible punishment on the Day when their tongues and hands and feet will testify against them about what they were doing. On that Day Allah will pay them in full what is due to them, and they will know that Allah is the Clear Truth❩ An-Nur: 23-25; there is both advice and a warning in the story of "The slander" (Hadith about Ifk).

The Advice of The Prophet ﷺ With Regards to Women

The men of the Quraish were so severe to their women; some used to harm them physically. But, as for the Prophet ﷺ, he had never hit a woman nor a servant in his life; he ﷺ used to say: "Be conscious of Allah in your conduct with women", "Treat your women well". He ﷺ used to feel extremely angry when upon hearing that a woman had been beaten up by her husband.

81

Abdullah bin Zam'ah said: "It is not wise for anyone of you to lash his wife like a slave, for he might sleep with her the same evening"[1].

'Aishah ♣ has said: "The Messenger of Allah ♣ never beat anyone with his hand; neither a woman nor a servant, but only in the case when he had been fighting in the cause of Allah, and then he never took revenge for anything, unless those things made inviolable by Allah were made violable; then he would take revenge for the sake of Allah, the Exalted and Glorious"[2].

Iyas bin Abdullah bin Abu Dhubab reported the Prophet ♣ as saying: "Do not beat Allah's handmaidens", but when Umar came to the Messenger of Allah and said: Women have become emboldened towards their husbands[3]", he (the Prophet) granted them the permission to beat them. Then many women came to the family of the Messenger of Allah, complaining against their husbands. So he ♣ said: "Many women have gone to Muhammad's family, complaining against their

---

[1] Agreed upon by all the scholars.
[2] Transmitted by Ahmad and Muslim.
[3] Al-Baghawi said: "In this Hadith, there is proof that beating women is legal when rejecting the rights of marriage, and the arrangement of this issue of "beating" in the Sunnah and the Qur'an shows that the Prophet ♣ forbid beating women before the Verse was revealed, then when some women became emboldened, he ♣ permitted their beating, and the Revelation supported his command; however when men abused this command, he ♣ explained that although the beating was legal, as a punishment for any of their mal-actions, to develop their patience over any of their bad morals. However, avoidance of resorting to beating is better and more acceptable; and it is also reported that Imam Ashafi'i supports this view. (from "Sharh Sunnah" 9/187).

husbands. They are not the best among you"[1]. Bahz bin Hakim said that his father quoted his grand father as saying: "I said: 'O Messenger of Allah! How should we approach our wives and how should we leave them?' He replied: 'Approach your tilt when or how you will, give her (your wife) food when you take food, clothe her when you clothe yourself, do not revile her face, and do not beat her'".

In preserving the dignity of women, Islam was not content only with stopping harm from reaching her, rather, the Prophet ﷺ had insisted on the following of his Sunnah in entertaining her, ensuring her happiness, and attracting what pleases her and delights her within the laws of Allah ﷻ. 'Aishah ؓ said: "I used to play with the dolls in the presence of the Prophet, and my (girl) friends also used to play with me. When the Prophet ﷺ used to enter (my dwelling place) they used to hide themselves, but the Prophet would call them back to join me and play with me"[2].

'Aishah ؓ also reported: "When the Prophet ﷺ arrived after the expedition to Tabuk or Khaybar, a draught raised one end of a curtain which hung in front of my store-room, revealing some dolls which belonged to me. He asked: 'What are these?' I replied: 'My dolls'. Among them he saw a horse with wings made of rags, so he asked: What is this I see among them?' I replied: 'A horse'. He asked: 'What are these that it has on it?' I

---

[1] Transmitted by Ibn Maajah, Addarami and Abu Dawud, and it was authenticated by Ibn Hibban and Al-Hakim, and supported by Adhahabi.

[2] Agreed upon by all scholars.

replied: 'Two wings'. He asked: 'A horse with two wings?' I replied: 'Have you not heard that Sulaiman (Solomon) had horses with wings?' She then added: 'Thereupon the Messenger of Allah laughed so heartily that I could see his molar teeth'"[1].

'Aishah ﷻ also reported: "Once I saw the Messenger of Allah at the door of my house, while some Ethiopians were playing in the mosque (displaying their skill with spears). He ﷺ was screening me with his Rida' (garment covering the upper part of the body) so as to enable me to see their display. I continued watching till I was satisfied. So you may deduce from this event how a little girl who is eager to enjoy amusement should be treated in this respect…"[2].

She ﷻ said in another narration that once the Prophet came to the house on 'Id day, and she was in the company of two Ansari girls who were singing songs about the battles of the day of Bu'ath (the battles that took place before Islam between Al-Aws and Al-Khazraj tribes), and since there was only just one room, he ﷺ laid himself on the bed and turned his back to them. But when Abu Bakr walked in, he ﷻ said protesting: "A musical instrument of Satan in the house of the Messenger of Allah!", the Prophet ﷺ said to him: "Leave them, Abu Bakr, for every nation has an 'Id (i.e. festival) and this day is our 'Id"[3].

---

[1] Transmitted by Abu Dawud.
[2] Agreed upon and transmitted by the majority of scholars.
[3] Transmitted by Al-Bukhari.

The Permitted Entertainment at a Wedding Feast

'Aishah ◈ said that she had prepared a lady, as a bride for an Ansari man, so the Prophet ◈ said, "O 'Aishah! Haven't you got any form of amusement (during the marriage ceremony), as the Ansar like amusement?"[1].

Muhammad bin Hatib Al-Jumahi ◈ has said: "The Prophet ◈ said: 'The distinction between what is lawful and what is unlawful is like the difference between a song and a tambourine at a wedding."[2]

'Amir bin S'ad ◈ reported: "I walked into a wedding attended by Qaradha bin Ka'b and abu Mas'ud Al-Ansari, while some maids were singing; and I said: 'O Companions of the Prophet and people of Badr[3]! Why is this taking place in your presence?' so, they replied: "Take a seat if you want to listen with us, otherwise you may go; indeed amusement has been permitted for us at weddings"[4].

A word of caution: It should be understood that this permitted amusement relates to the sound of the tambourine (which has bell sound), or young maids

---

[1] Transmitted by Al-Bukhari.

[2] Transmitted by Attirmidhi, Annassa'i, ibn Maajah, Imam Ahmad, and Al-Hakim; and it was regarded as a sound Hadith by Al-Albani in "Tahqiq Al-Mishkat" (2/943).

[3] Referring to their high status in Islam, because they attended the Great Battle of Badr alongside the Prophet ◈.

[4] Transmitted by Annassa'i, and it is a sound narration.

singing acceptable poetry (or lyrics), in contrast to the use of prohibited, idolatrous words, as in the songs of worldly, seductive singers and provocative music that people in our time have become infatuated with; we ask Allah to grant us well-being.

The Prophet's domestic life, among his wives, shows the best example of friendly relations, gentleness, amiability, comfort and support; as he ﷺ said: ""The best of you is he who is best to his family, and I am the best among you to my family"[1].

'Aishah ؓ was asked: "What was the work of the Messenger of Allah in his house?", she replied: "He was at the service of his family, until he went out for Salat". i.e. he ﷺ used to help by doing domestic work with his wives. She ؓ also said: "He used to repair his clothes, milk the sheep, and serve himself"[2].

It was out modesty (and simplicity) towards his wife, 'Aishah ؓ that he ﷺ used to race with her when she was on a journey with him; she ؓ said: "While I was on a journey along with the Messenger of Allah ﷺ: I had a race with him (the Prophet) and I overtook him on my feet. When I became bigger, I had another race with him

---

[1] Transmitted by Attirmidhi, Addarami and ibn Maajah; and it was authenticated by Al-Albani.
[2] Transmitted by Imam Ahmad, and Al-Bukhari in "Al-Adab Al-Mufrad", and Abu Na'im in Al-Hilyah. It was authenticated by Al-Albani.

(the Prophet), but he overtook me. He said: This is for that (last) overtaking"[1].

Anas ﷺ said, in his Hadith about Safiyyah ﷺ, that the Prophet ﷺ used to carry her goods in a woolen wrap, and would go close to his mount, putting his knee forward for Safiyyah to step on, for her to mount the camel".

The Companions of the Prophet ﷺsaid: "We have not seen anyone more merciful to children than the Prophet ﷺ"[2].

The Prophet ﷺ said in his farewell sermon: "Be conscious of Allah in your conduct with women; you have taken them with Allah's protection, and you have married them in the name of Allah"[3]. And in another narration: Amr ﷺ heard the Prophet ﷺ say in his farewell address, on the eve of his Last Pilgrimage, after he had glorified and praised Allah ﷺ; he cautioned his followers: "Listen! Treat women kindly; they are like prisoners in your hands. Beyond this, you do not owe anything to them. Should they be guilty of any flagrant misbehaviour, you may remove them from your beds, and beat them, but do not inflict upon them any severe punishment. Then should they obey you, do not have recourse to anything else against them. Listen! You have your rights upon your wives and they have their rights upon you. Your right is that they shall not allow anyone

---

[1] Transmitted by Imam Ahmed and Abu Dawud, and was authenticated by Al-Albani.
[2] Transmitted by Muslim.
[3] Transmitted by Muslim.

you dislike to trample your bed and do not permit those whom you dislike to enter your home. Their right is that you should treat them well in the matter of food and clothing"[1].

The Prophet ﷺ said: "Among the believers, who show the most perfect faith, are those who have the best disposition, and are kindest to their families"[2].

The Prophet ﷺ also said: "I advise you to take care of women, for they are created from a rib and the most crooked portion of the rib is its upper part; if you try to straighten it, it will break, and if you leave it, it will remain crooked, so I urge you to take care of women"[3].

The Prophet's ﷺ last advice was to say few words, which he ﷺ kept repeating: " Salat! Salat! (A reminder of the importance of Salat) and your wives: do not charge them above their ability; be conscious of Allah in your treatment to them, they are in your hands – prisoners – you took a pledge with Allah, and married them, in His Name"[4].

Allah ﷻ said: ﴿A Messenger has come to you from among yourselves. Your suffering is distressing to him; he is deeply concerned for you; he is gentle and merciful to the believers﴾. At-Tawbah: 128.

---

[1] Transmitted by Attirmidhi and Ibn Maajah.
[2] Transmitted by Attirmidhi.
[3] Transmitted by Al-Bukhari and Muslim, on the authority of Abu Hurairah ؓ.
[4] Transmitted by Annassa'i, and ibn Maajah.

The Abolition of all Jahili[1] Customs at Funerals

Women have been affected, in a positive way, by the culture and morality of Islam, and have avoided distasteful Jahili habits or blind imitation. The first thing a Muslim woman was taught was to be patient in times of calamity; indeed, Islam has prevented her from practicing bad habits, such as tearing her clothes or hitting her face, etc, following the death of a dear or kind person from her family.

The Prophet ﷺ took the pledge of allegiance from the women of Madinah, "on the condition that, when mourning, they do not wail and lament, nor scratch their faces, nor tear the front of their garments, nor curse themselves, nor expose their hair, nor shout or raise their voices"[2].

That pledge of allegiance was bestowed upon all female believers, and became one of the principles of their Religion, and an important aspect of their faith. They have understood how Allah ﷻ has promised to greatly reward patient men and women; from Allah's words:

❲The steadfast will be paid their rewards in full without any reckoning❳ Az-Zumar: 10.

Allah ﷻ has also said about the steadfast:

---

[1] Jahiliyah is the pre-Islamic era when people were worshipping idols.
[2] "Attabaqat Al-Kubra" by Ibn Sa'd (7/3-6).

《Those are the people who will have Blessings and Mercy from their Lord; they are the ones who are guided》 Al-Baqarah: 157.

They have heard about the Prophet's ﷺ reporting of the words of Allah: "Allah says, I have nothing to give but Paradise as a reward to my believer slave, who, if I cause his dear friend (or relative) to die, remains patient (and hopes for Allah's Reward)[1].

They have listened and understood all these revelations, which have become a comfort to their souls and their hearts, then the Sunnah of the Prophet ﷺ came with a set of advices and restrictions to cancel and annihilate all the Jahili habits:

Abu Malik Al-Ash'ari ﷺ said: the Messenger of Allah ﷺ said: "Among my people there are four characteristics belonging to pre-Islamic period which they have not abandoned: boasting of high rank, reviling other peoples' genealogies, seeking rain by stars, and wailing". And he (further) said: "If a wailing woman does not repent before she dies, she will be made to stand on the Day of Resurrection wearing a garment of pitch and a shirt like mange"[2].

There was more wailing than weeping (grieving and expressing sorrow audibly); Ibn Al-'Arabi said: "Wailing was practiced in pre-Islamic times; women used to stand facing each other screaming, throwing dust on their heads and hitting their faces".

---

[1] Transmitted by Al-Bukhari.
[2] Transmitted by Muslim and Al-Baihaqi.

Umm 'Atiyah ◈ said: "We gave a pledge of allegiance to the Prophet ◈, and the he recited verse (60.12) to me; that they will not associate anything in worship with Allah. And he also prevented us from wailing and lamenting over the dead"[1].

The Prophet ◈ said, "He who slaps his cheeks, tears his clothes and follows the ways and traditions of the Days of Ignorance is not one of us."[2]

Abu Burda bin Abu Musa said: "Abu Musa was suffering some pain and fell unconscious with his head on the thigh of his wife. one woman in his family screamed, but he could not reply to her, so when he came around, he said: "I am not with those whom the Prophet ◈ has distanced himself from; so he ◈ declared he was free from being responsible for a woman who screams while grieving, a woman who shaves her head, or one who tears the front of her garment"[3].

Usayd bin Abu Usayd, reported on the authority of a woman who took an oath of allegiance to the Prophet: "One of the oaths which the Messenger of Allah ◈ received from us about virtue was that we would not disobey him in it (virtue): that we would not scratch our face, nor wail, nor tear the front of the garments nor dishevel our hair"[4].

---

[1] Transmitted by Al-Bukhari and Muslim.
[2] Transmitted by Al-Bukhari and Muslim.
[3] Transmitted by Al-Bukhari, Muslim, Annassa'i, and Al-Baihaqi.
[4] Transmitted by Abu Dawud and Al-Baihaqi, and it was authenticated by Al-Albani.

Umm Salamah reported: "When Abu Salamah ﷺ died I said to myself: 'He is a stranger in a strange land, I shall weep for him in a manner that would be talked of'. I made preparation for weeping for him when a woman from the upper side of the city came there who intended to help me (in weeping). She happened to come across the Messenger of Allah ﷺ who said: 'Do you intend to bring the devil back into a house from which Allah has (already) driven him out?' (He ﷺ repeated it). I (Umm Salamah), therefore, refrained from weeping and did not weep"[1]. She ﷺ meant by stranger the fact that Abu Salamah ﷺ was of the people of Makkah, yet died in Al-Madinah.

Gathering For Mourning Is Makrooh[2]

Among the (right) guidance of Islam with regards to Funerals is that it considers the gathering of mourners in a specific place (a house, cemetery, or mosque) as disliked, following the Hadith, on the authority of Jarir bin Abdullah Al-Bajali ﷺ who said: "We used to consider the gathering of the family of the deceased, and the preparation of food after burying him as a type of wailing". Anawawi has said: "The gathering for mourning was defined by Ashafi'i and other scholars as Makrooh. They meant to gather so that the family of the deceased could assemble in one place and people could visit them to mourn. Scholars have said they should, rather, carry on with their lives and activities, and

---

[1] Transmitted by Muslim.
[2] Reprehensible, unpleasant, disliked

92

whoever meets them, should present his condolences to them, and this applies to men and women alike".

The Concession For Weeping Without Wailing

Islam has permitted people to ease their suffering, for the loss of their beloved ones through their tears; Usama bin Zaid ؏ has said: "A son of one of the daughters of the Prophet was dying, so she sent a person to call the Prophet ؛. He ؛ sent her a message: "Whatever Allah takes is for Him, and whatever He gives is for Him; everything has a limited, fixed term (in this world); so she should be patient and hope for Allah's reward." She then sent for him again, swearing that he should come. The Prophet ؛ got up, and so did Mu'adh bin Jabal, Ubai bin Ka'b and 'Ubadah bin As-Samit. When he ؛ entered (the house), they gave the child to Allah's Apostle after he had stopped breathing. (The sub-narrator said: I think he said, "...as if it was a waterskin.)" The Prophet ؛ started weeping whereupon Sa'd bin 'Ubadah said, "Do you weep?" The Prophet replied, "Allah is merciful only to those of His slaves who are merciful (to others)"[1].

Anas ؏ said: "We went with Messenger of Allah ؛ to the blacksmith, Abu Saif, who was the husband of the wet-nurse of Ibrahim (the son of the Prophet). The Prophet ؛ picked up Ibrahim, kissed him and smelt him. Later we entered Abu Saif's house, when Ibrahim was breathing his last breaths, and the eyes of the Messenger

---

[1] Transmitted Al-Bukhari, Muslim, Abu Dawud, Annassa'i, Ibn Maajah, Al-Baihaqi and Imam Ahmad.

of Allah began to shed tears. 'Abdur Rahman bin 'Auf said, "O Messenger of Allah! Even you are weeping!" He ﷺ replied, "O Ibn 'Auf, this is mercy." Then he ﷺ wept more and said, "The eyes are shedding tears and the heart is grieving, and we will not say anything except what pleases our Lord, O Ibrahim! Indeed we are grieved by your separation."[1]

'Aishah ؓ said: "The Prophet ﷺ entered the house of 'Uthman bin Madh'un who lay dead, so he ﷺ uncovered the face of 'Uthman, leant towards him and kissed him, and wept until tears were dripping on his cheeks"[2].

The Guidance of Islam in Mourning The Deceased

It is a part of patience that a woman should abstain from using cosmetics when mourning her son or others if the period is not exceeding three days, except in the case of the death of her husband; then she may mourn for a period of four months and ten days, excluding the pregnant woman.   Hamid bin Nafi' has said: I was informed by Zainab Bint Abi Salamah, who said: "When Umm Habibah bint Abi Sufyan was informed of her father's death, she asked for perfume and rubbed it over her arms and said, "I am not in need of perfume, but I have heard the Prophet ﷺ saying, "It is not lawful for a lady who believes in Allah and the Last Day to mourn for more than three days, except for her husband for whom the (mourning) period is four months and ten days."

---

[1] Transmitted by Al-Bukhari, Muslim and Al-Baihaqi.
[2] Transmitted by Attirmidhi, and Al-Baihaqi.

94

During this period of mourning the husband, and out of respect for his right to fidelity, Islam instructs a woman mourner to avoid anything that makes her look attractive and desirable (for marriage); of which there are four things:

(1) Perfumery

(2) Avoiding the use cosmetics for beauty[1], or wearing clothes for embellishment or jewellery, or even the finger ring according to the opinion of the majority of the scholars.

(3) Not to wear the Niqab (the veil that covers the whole face except the eyes), but if she has to cover her face, she may throw a wrap over her head, the way the woman in Hajj does.

(4) Not to spend the night outside her place; the mourning wife should observe the house where her husband died, whether it is his property, or rented, or borrowed, except when there is a good excuse[2].

Islam Refines The Feelings of Women

Islam has reached the hearts of women, removing resentment, by purifying it from any hatred (of the

---

[1] However she cleanse herself by: manicure, clipping her armpit, bathing…
[2] See "Al-Mughni" by Ibn Qudama (7/ 518-522).

95

avenger), raging inside their chests. They were, indeed, expressing their rancour and disapproval of their situation, until Allah ﷻ sent down His Revelation about Al-Qisas (Punishment, Penal legislation) in this world and in the Hereafter, and rescued the Arab nation from social classes, and constant feuds. Yet, Allah ﷻ has joined their hearts together, and they became brothers by His blessing; He ﷻ turned their hatred into amity, and resentment into goodwill.

The Prophet ﷺ used to curse those raising the call for Jahiliyah[1], and has said: "Whoever slaps his face or tears the front of his dress, or uses the calls of the period of ignorance, is not from us"[2]. Such a call of Jahiliyah is when a man or woman calls for revenge, so that the armies raise their banners immediately, and set out to meet in (bloody) combat, giving total support for an individual, whether he/she was an oppressor or oppressed.

Was there a heart that was filled with hatred towards the Prophet ﷺ, and his family, more than the heart of Hind, daughter of 'Utbah? Some members of her family were killed, and the Prophet ﷺ had condemned her to death, on the Day of the Conquest of Makkah, for mutilating the body of his cousin, Hamzah ﷺ in the battle of Uhud; she cut open his abdomen when he died, pulled out his liver; it was one of the most evil inclinations of Jahiliyah. Yet, Hind, disguised in a veil, came to pledge allegiance to the Prophet ﷺ and said: "O Messenger of Allah! All praise to

---

[1] The Pre-Islamic period of ignorance characterised by polytheism, and other immoral and unjust practices.

[2] Transmitted by Al-Bukhari, Muslim and others.

Allah who revealed the religion He chooses for Himself. O Muhammad! I am a woman who believes in Allah and His Messenger". Then, she removed her veil and said: "I am Hind, daughter of 'Utbah". The Prophet ﷺ said: "Welcome to you", so she replied: "By Allah! There were no weak people on earth that I wanted so much to see disgraced than you and your people, but now I want to see that you are the most honoured on earth." It is, indeed, the way of Allah and His Religion that hatred and repulsion should be removed from the hearts.

Just as Allah ﷻ has purified the hearts of women from hatred, so He ﷻ has also removed from them the cover of ignorance and falsehood; she has become free from any false creed or evil presentiments of deception. She has learnt that Allah ﷻ has prevented even His most pure slaves from having access to the Unknown (which He ﷻ alone knows); so she has never asked for or tried to discover it; she turned her back on (all) the falsehood of fortunetellers and their practices. She has become aware that the command is for Allah alone; that He ﷻ alone can convert a heart, and change the situation of any individual.

Disproof of The Deviation of Absolute Equality Between Men and Women

Allah ﷻ has said:

❴male and female are not the same❵ Al-'Imran: 36.

After announcing its clear position on the humanity and dignity of women, Islam has looked into her nature and what is convenient for her in life's activities; so it has protected her from all that contradicts her nature or prevents her from carrying out her complete message (task) in society. For this reason, Islam has assigned, her in particular, some rules –not man – and at the same time, it has reprieved her from some religious and social obligations, such as the Jumu'ah Salat (Friday prayer), the Ihram code in Hajj, and Jihad in times other than when it is a general obligation, and other cases among which will be discussed later insha Allah, which are in harmony with her instinct and nature.

Allah 🕮 has said:

《Mankind! We created you from a male and a female》 Al-Hujurat: 13.

and He 🕮 explained this in the following verse:

《He created you from a single self, and produced its mate from it》 Az-Zumar: 6.

Therefore, these verses prove that the existence of the first woman was related to the existence of man; for she was a branch from him. This was a universal and a divine pre-ordainment of Allah 🕮. He 🕮 created woman – in her first existence – from man, and then came the sublime legislation came, revealed by Allah 🕮 to be practiced on earth, taking into consideration this Divine Command in all the aspects of a woman's life.

Allah 🕮 has made man a guardian of woman, and made her rely on him in all her affairs; He 🕮 said:

《Men have charge of women》 An-Nisa': 34.

Therefore, any attempt to equate woman to man, in all aspects of life, could not be achieved, because of the differences between the two (types): first, with regards to the Divine Predestination, and second, Divine Revelation, completely opposing such an idea. Because of these powerful and critical differences, the Prophet ﷺ cursed those imitating the other gender (male or female), for there is no doubt that the reason for this damnation is the attempt of one person to resemble the other in order to eliminate any differences, which are, in fact, distinct and irrevocable.

Allah ﷻ said:

⟪Do you have males and He females; that is a most unfair division⟫ An-Najm: 21

(i.e. it is unfair because of the inequality of the two shares, as the preference is of men over women). The wife of 'Imran realized the distinction of gender when she gave birth to Mary(Mariam), as Allah ﷻ said:

⟪When she gave birth, she said: "My Lord! I have given birth to a girl – and Allah knew very well what she had given birth to – male and female are not the same⟫ Al-'Imran: 36.

The wife of 'Imran said: **⟪male and female are not the same⟫** and she is undoubtedly truthful, while the polytheists and their followers say: **⟪male and female are the same⟫**.

The Necessity of Fitrah[1] In The Lifestyle of a Married Couple

Islam is the religion of Fitrah, so what has been determined by Islamic legislation, in dividing matrimonial duties between man and woman, is in accordance with this Fitrah. Allah ﷻ has given preference to man by nature of his Physical strength and intellect, with which he has acquired the ability to earn the living and defend his family and nation. He was consequently obliged to support his family, and thus men have been given custody of women; they assume both particular and public leadership; no special nor general system would last without it. From the requirements of the Fitrah is in allowing women time for pregnancy, breastfeeding, nursing the children, raising them, and managing the housekeeping; the Prophet ﷺ said: "Everyone of you is a guardian and is responsible for his charge; the ruler is a guardian and is responsible for his subjects; the man is a guardian in his family and responsible for his charges; a woman is a guardian of her husband's house and responsible for her charges". So contemplate on how he ﷺ confined her role to in the home of her husband.

Only an ignorant or haughty individual would argue about Allah's preference of man to woman, in the system of Fitrah. And whoever examines the character of women, whose Fitrah is sound and undamaged, will find that the issue of preference is established within their nature; and the surest evidence for that is the fact

---

[1] Inborn nature; instinct induced in humans by Allah ﷻ.

100

that most women would prefer their first new born child to be a male, and they boast among themselves about that.

The Evidence of This Preference

Allah ﷻ has said: **《Men have charge of women because Allah has preferred one》** i.e. men **《above the other》** i.e. women; then He ﷻ said: **《men have a degree above them》** Al-Baqarah 228. this is because males have an innate natural power, and dignity; as for females, they have some natural weaknesses as it is witnessed by every rational individual, and it would only be denied by an arrogant.

Allah ﷻ has pointed to that when He ﷻ said: **《What! Someone brought up among pretty trinkets who cannot produce a cogent argument!》** Az-Zukhruf: 19. He ﷻ disclaimed and rebuked the polytheists, in this holy verse, when they attributed a child to Him ﷻ; for that is not proper for Him ﷻ. They ascribed to Him the weaker of the two; since females are "brought up among pretty trinkets", using all kind of beautification and jewellery. But men disregard adornment. Al-Alusi has said: "This verse indicates that being given an upbringing with adornment and tenderness is a sign of weakness; therefore, a man has to avoid over-dressing, to reject it haughtily, to deem himself above it, and live as 'Umar bin Al-Khattab said: "Be rough in your dressing, and rough in your eating…" and if one wants to beautify himself, he could do it with decency and modesty".

Allah ﷻ has said:

《Do you have males and He females; that is a most unfair division》 An-Najm: 21,

this division was unfair because the female is innately and naturally shorter than the male, so they (the polytheists) ascribed this weaker gender to Him ﷻ, and attributed the males for themselves, as Allah ﷻ said:

《They allot to Allah what they themselves dislike》 An-Nahl: 62 (i.e. the females.)

Allah ﷻ said:

《When any of them is given the good news of the very thing which he himself has ascribed to the All-Merciful》 (i.e. the female,) **《his face darkens and he is furious》** Az-Zukhruf: 17.

All these verses prove that the female is incomplete in terms of her nature and innate character, and that the male is better and more complete, Allah ﷻ said:

《Has He chosen daughters over sons, what is the matter with you, how do you reach your judgment》 As-Saffat: 153-154;

《Has your Lord honoured you with sons and Himself taken the angels as daughters?》 Al-Isra': 40.

Among the evidence that the female is naturally weaker is the fact that the first woman was created from the rib of the first man; so her origin is only from a part of him.

Ibn Kathir said explaining the verse:

❰What! Someone brought up among pretty trinkets who cannot produce a cogent argument!❱ Az-Zukhruf: 19

that woman has a defect, and she makes up for it by wearing ornaments from a young age, and when she argues, she falls short of explaining herself, or rather is incapable of logical expression. So how could anyone who has these shortcomings, be related to Allah 🕮? A female is short, both in her outward appearance and in her inner side; that is lacking physical and mental concepts. So her outward deficiency is treated by using adornments and anything similar, to repair any shortcomings; as for her mental deficiency, she is weak and unable to triumph when she needs to, falling short of expression and determination"[1]. This example is not taken from a few rare women, because judgment is not derived from rare or exceptional ones.

The Prophet 🕮 said to some women that he 🕮 passed by: "O women! Give alms, as I have seen that the majority of the dwellers of Hell-Fire were you (women)." They asked, "Why is it so, O Messenger of Allah?" He replied, "You curse frequently and are ungrateful to your husbands. I have not seen anyone more deficient in intelligence and religion than you. A cautious sensible man could be led astray by some of you"[2]. Shaikh Abdullah bin Hamid said: "This is an authentic and clear

---

[1] See "Al-Insaf fi Masa'il al-Khilaf" (Fairness in the Issues of Differences) by ibn Al-Anbari (1/99).
[2] Transmitted by Al-Bukhari.

text about the deficiency of a woman's (practice of her) religion and intelligence compared to that of a man, because necessarily, those who only perform Salat some of the time (in their life) are not equal to those who perform Salat all their lives, or those who can only fast for some days, in the month of Ramadan, with those who can fast the whole month! In the rest of the Hadith: "The women asked, "O Messenger of Allah! What is deficient in our intelligence and religion?" He said, "Is not the evidence of two women equal to the witness of one man?" They replied in the affirmative. He said, "This is the deficiency in her intelligence. Isn't it true that a woman can neither pray nor fast during her menses?" The women replied in the affirmative. He said, "This is the deficiency in her religion." So whoever tries to equate between man and woman has indeed perpetrated an offence against Islam, and taken a deviated path".

The Guardianship of Man is Organizational Not Arbitrary:

Abu Hurairah ⚭ has said: The Prophet ﷺ said: "Everyone of the children of Adam is a master; a man is master of his family, and a woman is master of her house"[1].

The guardianship of men over women is a principle of organization which is prerequisite for the building of society and the harmony of its social conventions. Similarly, for presidents and leaders; it is a necessity

---

[1] Transmitted by ibn Sunni, and was authenticated by Al-Albani.

condition for an Islamic or any other society. It is sinful for a Muslim to avoid doing this, for whatever reason; for the nature of man qualifies him to be the leader or guardian. He is more powerful than a woman, and more able to tackle the big problems in life, and assume its responsibilities. All big projects are directed by men, and the top leadership of the state is assumed by men. Therefore, it can be seen that major issues are generally and successfully conducted by men, and it is rare for a woman to succeed in similar tasks, unless there is a man supervising it.

Nevertheless, the scope of man's guardianship does not lessen the sanctity of women or their dignity; for this is why the Qur'an never stated: "Men are masters of women", instead, it chooses the more accurate term "qawwamun", (supporters) to reflect a sublime and constructive meaning; that they (men) are reformers who are just, not arbitrary nor despotic. The extent of guardianship is, therefore, confined to the benefit of the marital house, the rights of the spouse, and the following of the Commandments of Allah ﷻ. Man does not have this right to interfere in the wife's independent ownership; she should only obey him within in the limits of what Allah ﷻ has decreed; if he instructs her to insubordination (beyond the limits of Islam; a sin), then as Allah's Messenger ﷺ has said, "A creature is not to be obeyed when it involves disobedience to the Creator", and as long as a woman respects the boundaries of Allah ﷻ, and the rights of her husband, then she is due all the dignity and respect from him. In fact, a man's good relation and moral conduct with his wife are among the greatest standards of perfection and soundness in religion: The Prophet ﷺ said: "The most perfect Muslim in the matter of faith is one who has excellent behaviour; and the best among you are those who behave best towards their wives".

A statement from Dr. August Forrell, titled "The ruling of a woman":

"A woman feels that she needs her husband's protection, and this feeling deeply affects deeply her emotions. A woman cannot experience happiness unless she feels respect from her husband; she also wants to perceive in him the best example, in many aspects: physical power, courage, sacrifice, intellectual superiority, and any other good virtue; or else, he could easily fall victim to her command and her control, or they could even cast with a feeling of aversion and coldness towards each other. It is only when an illness comes to afflict her husband, thus stirring her sympathy, and enabling her to nurse and to provide the care that he needs. A woman's rule could never bring happiness at home, because it contradicts the natural fact that a man rules a woman with his insight, intellect and will, while she rules him with her heart and affection".

Differences Between Men And Women

Devoting The Prophethood and The Message to Men and Not to Women

The message of Islam is the call to Allah by word and deed; one usually has to face enemies and opponents who are inclined to defend their worldly interests, or imitate their ancestors, unreasonably and blindly. For this cause one must be prepared to suffer persecution, harm, imprisonment torture, or even death.

The Message is established by one's truthfulness in giving evidence, and one's insight in holding an argument or conducting a debate. This prevents falsehood from prevailing, and drives away doubt and suspicion, with the truth; the return of light after darkness. By Allah! Only men are fully able to implement this because they were born for the task, while women cannot carry this responsibility because they were not made for it. It is for this reason that Allah ﷻ selected men as the best of people (i.e. the Prophets ﷺ) able to deliver the Message: **《Your Lord creates and chooses whatever He wills》** Al-Qasas: 68, and He ﷻ said: **《We sent none before you but men inspired with revelation》** Yusuf: 109.

Along with prophethood, which was only assigned to men, there are other (unique) categories for men:

- Reserving and assigning the command to perform Jihad for men; 'Aishah ؓ said: "O Messenger of Allah! We (women) see Jihad as the best of all deeds, shouldn't we participate in Jihad, along with you? He ﷺ replied: The best and the most superior Jihad for women is (to perform) Hajj which is (subsequently) accepted by Allah"[1].

- Assigning ethical and educational responsibility, primarily, to man; Allah ﷻ said: **❴O you believers! Safeguard yourselves and your families from a Fire whose fuel is people and stones❵** Attahrim: verse 6.

- Regarding the testimony of woman as half that of man before a judge. In fact, Islam made the minimum number of testimonies, which confirms the rights to their people, as the testimony of two sound men, or one man and two women; as Allah ﷻ has said: **❴Two men among you should act as witnesses, but if there are not two men, then man and two women with whom you are satisfied as witnesses; then if one of them forgets, the other can remind her❵** Al-Baqarah: verse 282.

Thus, this clear evidence for the suitability of men to work outside the home rather than women. The Holy verse shows that woman's primary function is to stay behind to care for the affairs of her house, and to raise her children. In certain circumstances, if she finds herself compelled to mingle with men, in the working field, (in a matter of necessity only) then she has to observe extreme reservation, and should not (or rarely) attend men's meetings, financial contracts or buying and

---

[1] Transmitted by Al-Bukhari.

selling transactions. However, if she does attend some of them, she would be less informed to understand the whole of the subject, and therefore, her testimony would not be complete. So, it is necessary to add a woman (like her) in her testimony to recover whatever is missing in the statement; as Allah 🕮 has said: **〈then if one of them forgets, the other can remind her〉**, because people's rights need to be asserted and confirmed.

It is because of this that most scholars do not accept testimonies from women in criminal cases, simply because many woman usually look after their homes, and do not have a chance to attend disputes which could end in violence, etc; and she rarely stays to witness (with her eyes) the crime of killing; if she does not run away, she usually closes her eyes, screams or faints (sometimes). Therefore, how could she provide a descriptive statement about crime, criminals, or even a crime weapon, etc? It is an indisputable fact that a legal punishment (Hudud) has to be averted by suspicion; the testimony of woman for a crime is surrounded with doubt: the fact of her inability to describe the crime, due to her nervous psychological state when it took place.

Nevertheless, Shari'ah does accept the testimony of a woman (on her own), in matters that are not known to others, especially men; it has been decided that her sole testimony is accepted to confirm childbirth, puberty, or any defect in a woman's body, and also in breastfeeding. 'Uqbah bin Al-Harith said that he had married Umm Yahya bint Abu Ihab. He explained, "A black slave-lady once came and said, 'I suckled you both' So I mentioned that to the Prophet who turned his face aside." Uqba continued by saying, "I went to the other side and told the Prophet about it (again) saying that she was a liar. He ﷺ replied, "How can you (keep her as your wife) when the lady has said that she (once) suckled both of you (i.e. you and your wife?)" So, the Prophet ﷺ ordered him to divorce her!

The Inheritance of a Woman is Less Than That of a Man, in General

Islam has confirmed a share for woman in inheritance, which should not be bypassed at all; for Allah ﷺ has said: ❨There is a share for men and a share for women from what is left by parents and those nearest related, whether, the property be small or large – a legal share❩ An-Nisa': verse 7, but man carries the family line (source) of the lineage. So the share differs in its regulations under different conditions:

Allah ﷺ has stated in this Holy verse that He ﷺ has given preference to the male of the female, in the issue of legacy, to prevent there being a deviation from the Truth; and whoever equates between the two (males and females) in this matter, has surely deviated from the Right Path. Allah ﷺ has explained that He is ﷺ The Most Knowing of the regulations, interests and everything that concerns His creation: ❨And Allah is Aware of everything❩, and the wisdom for this preference is evident, since the issue concerns the justice in distributing the responsibilities among His creation. The weak and deficient are generally reliant upon the strong and powerful; so, therefore, it is necessary for men

110

to fully support their women, and provide for all their needs; Allah ﷻ said: ❨**and because they spend (to support them) from their means**❩ An-Nisa': verse 34. The heritage wealth (money) was not produced by any of them both (husband or wife), they never strove to earn it (out of convention); but, it is rather a compulsory conveyance of property to man from Allah ﷻ, Whose Wisdom made it requisite that men are given preference to women in legacy. Men are always expected to be short o wealth, due to their providing support to their wives and children; they are required to pay the dowries to the wives; they have to spend in the event of any calamity; they provide for their poor relatives who inherit after them; their homes are open to their visitors. As for a woman, she is always expected to gain more; a day comes when a man proposes to marry her; he grants her a dowry as a gift for her; he then fully supports her and provides for all her needs, and she is not required to help in any way (with anything) with the expenses of her house and her children, even if she is wealthy. Her wealth, moreover, may increase if she invests it in commerce or in any other legal type of investment.

Therefore, preferring the one who is expected to live in shortage (man) to the one who is expected to live in prosperity (woman) – in terms of wealth – is a clear and wise reason, which is denied and rejected only by those for whom Allah has blinded (their insight) with Kufr (polytheism) and major sin (May Allah protects us from them). An example which should not be followed, is repeatedly quoted by atheists, who spare no effort to spread suspicions about the Divine Command of Allah; and He ﷻ said of them: ❨**And so judge between them** by what Allah has revealed and follow not their vain desires, but beware of them lest they turn you far away from some of that which Allah has sent down to you. And if they turn away, then know that Allah's Will is to punish them for some sins of theirs. And truly, most of people are disobedient to Allah. Do they seek the judgement of the Days of Ignorance? And who is better in judgement than Allah for a people who have firm faith》 Al-Ma'idah: 49-50, and He ﷻ also said: 《And wish not for things in which Allah has made some of you to excel others. For men there is reward for what they have earned, and for women there is reward for they have earned, and ask Allah for His Bounty. Surely, Allah is Ever All-Knower of everything》 An-Nisa': 32.

Scholars have agreed to judge as a disbeliever whoever allows (and permits the use of) equality in legacy between males and females, while it is clearly a subject of preference in the Book of Allah and the Sunnah of His Prophet; because it is a disbelief in part of the Revelation of Allah, and a deviation from the Shari'ah of Allah (to the command of the Taghut[1]), as Allah ﷻ has said: 《The only saying of the faithful believers, when they are called to Allah (His words, the Qur'an) and His Messenger, to judge between them, is that they say:

---

[1] The word Taghut covers wide range of meanings: It means anything worshipped other than the Real God (Allah), (i.e. all the false deities). It may be Satan, devils, idols, stones, the sun, stars, angels, human beings e.g. (Jesus, Messengers of Allah), who have all been falsely worshipped and taken as Taghuts. Likewise saints, graves, rulers, leaders, etc., have also been falsely worshipped, and wrongly followed.

"We hear and we obey". And such are the successful⟩, and He ⁜ also said: ⟨But no, by your Lord, they can have no Faith, until they make you (the Messenger of Allah) judge in all disputes between them, and find in themselves no resistance against your decisions, and accept (them) with full submission⟩ An-Nisa': verse 65.

Issue: Do parents have to treat equally between male and the female children with regards to giving gift?

The Prophet ⁜ said: "Act equally between your children when giving gifts; for I were to prefer one over the other, I would prefer (and be generous) to women"[1].

Shaikh Muhammad 'Umar Byunid has said: "The Islamic scholars have agreed on the permission of parent's gifts to their children, however they differed on the issue of preferring some children to the others, in offering presents, or when granting all the wealth to some and denying others".

The Hanafi, Shafi'i and Maliki schools state that equality among children is recommended, and that preference is reprehensible; (i.e. it is not legal to distinguish between the male and the female in this issue), therefore, a female should be given exactly as a male, and scholars have

---

[1] Transmitted by Sa'id bin Mansur, and Al-Baihaqi, on the authority of Ibn 'Abbass (who quoted directly from the Prophet ⁜). Ibn Hajar said: this Hadith has a sound chain of authorities, Fath Al-Bari (5/214).

mentioned, as evidence, that 'Aishah, the wife of the Prophet ﷺ once said, "Abu Bakr as-Siddiq gave me some palm trees, whose produce was twenty Awsuq, from his property at al-Ghaba. When he was dying, he said, "By Allah, little daughter, there is no one I would prefer to be wealthy, after I die, than you. There is no one whom it is more difficult for me to see poor, after I die than you. I gave you palm-trees whose produce was twenty Awsuq. Had you cut them and taken possession of them, they would have been yours, but today they are the property of the heirs"[1]. Ashafi'i mentioned a Hadith narrated by Annu'man bin Bashir ﷺ that the Prophet ﷺ said: "Act equally between your children; Act equally between your sons"[2].

There are many traditions of the Prophet ﷺ, in this context, which state that inequality between the children in the family is Haram since it leads inevitably to enmity and hatred among them, and eventually to the cut off relationships within families.

The Hanbali scholars and their followers state that no individual is permitted to prefer some of his children over others, when offering presents or distributing gifts; it should not be established like the division of the legacy. Imam Ahmed ibn Hanbal said that there should be no preference between the children, as long as there is no reason that requires it, and if there is a reason, then there is no objection to it; he said: "If some of them are specially preferred for a particular reason, because they are suffering from an illness or blindness, or if they were

---

[1] Transmitted by Imam Malik in Al-Muwatta'.
[2] Transmitted by Abu Dawud (2/362)

114

devoted to their studies, etc. However, sometimes they are out of favour, because of their immoral attitude and behaviour, so the parents should deny some of them any gifts, because otherwise, it would encourage them in their bad conduct and disobedience to Allah 🕮"[1].

The Hanbali scholars evidence is the Hadith by An-Nu'man bin Bashir who said that his father took him to the Messenger of Allah and said, "I have given this son of mine a slave." The Prophet asked, "Have you given all your sons alike?" He replied in the negative. The Prophet said, "Take back your gift then." Al-Bukhari, Muslim and ibn Majah all agreed that the reaction of the Prophet 🕮 (when he asked him to reconsider his action) meant that the gift was not valid; and in other narrations of this Hadith, the Prophet 🕮 was quoted as saying: "This is injustice".

Furthermore, Allah 🕮 has established the share of the male as that of two females in legacy; He 🕮 said: ❰**Allah instructs you regarding your children: A male receives the same as the share of two females**❱ An-Nisa': 11, so the Command of Allah should be implemented, and since the Hibah[2] can be so important and useful, it should be given according to the division of the legacy (i.e. male receives the same as the share of two females), because males always bare the burdens of life more than females. In marriage, a male is required to donate a dowry to the female and to assume all the expenses on the wife and the children, thus the need to

---

[1] See "Al-Mughni" by Ibn Kudamah (5/665).
[2] Also called 'Atiyah: the offering; anything given by the father to his children in his life (gifts, presents, money, etc.)

115

prefer him (in legacy) is justified. Allah ﷻ has considered all those issues when setting the share of the legacy; therefore, a male has to consider all this when distributing Hibah to his children. Allah ﷻ did not leave the distribution of wealth to anyone, but to Himself ﷻ, when He ﷻ said: ❨These are obligatory shares from Allah❩ An-Nissa': 11.

The narration of Abu Bakr does not oppose that of the Prophet ﷺ, and it should not be used as a proof against it; for it is possible that Abu Bakr had assigned a Hibah to his daughter 'Aishah ؓ because of her need for it and her inability to provide for herself, but also for her deserving status as the Mother of Believers, and the wife of the Messenger of Allah ﷺ. It is also likely that he ؓ granted that offering while he still intended to grant his other children as well, before his death. Therefore, the truth is that equality among the children is an obligation, however, some scholars have differed on how to establish it; Muhammad bin Al-Hasan, Ahmed, Ishaq and some Shafi'i scholars have said: "Justice recommends that the male be given the share of two females, as in legacy". As for the majority of scholars, they claim that there should be no difference in giving between the male and the female, and obviously this is the command for equality.

We see the opinion of the Hanbali scholars as the right one because of their strong evidence, which conform to this verse, and because they carefully explained the wisdom behind distinguishing between males and females, in terms of Islamic legislation and in their different levels of reasoning.

Assigning the authority to give divorce to the husband

It is referred to in the following Verses in the Qur'an: Allah ﷻ has said:

❮O Prophet! When any of you divorce women❯ Attalaq: 1;

❮or the one in charge of the marriage contract forgoes it❯ (Al-Baqarah: 235) i.e. the husband;

❮If you divorce them before you have touched them❯ (Al-Baqarah: 237);

❮Divorced women should wait by themselves for three menstrual cycles❯ (Al-Baqarah: 228);

❮and if he divorces his wife a third time, she is not Halal for him after that until she has married another man❯ (Al-Baqarah: 230).

The Muslims all agree that divorce is in the hands of the husband; he is the one to agree to and sign for it, if he wants to do so.

The wisdom behind granting man the right to cancel the marital contract

Women are like "fields" and "plantations" where sperm could be sown, the way grain is sown in the ground; as Allah ﷻ has said: ❮Your women are fertile fields for

117

you❩, and there is no doubt that since men possess the order of the "plantation", then they should not use it in a field which is unfit for it. It is for this reason that people of knowledge agreed to relate the child to the father and not to the mother; Allah ﷻ said: ❨**But the father of the child shall bear the cost of the mother's food and clothing on a reasonable basis**❩ Al-Baqarah: 232.

A man is usually the one who requests marriage from a woman, gives her the dowry and sets up the marital home.

It is the man who possesses the guardianship and the big responsibility in the family; it is his right to organize the affairs of the family.

It is the husband who supports his divorced wife during her 'Iddah[1] until it expires, and the period might take up to nine months, if he divorces her while she is pregnant, and so her 'Iddah ends when she gives birth.

It is the husband who supports all his children while they are in the custody of the mother, and the period might last seven years and more.

Assigning divorce to the hands of the judge is a means to adultery

rejecting the system of Islam and assigning the matter of divorce to the judge is a clear violation of the

---

[1] Prescribed period of waiting during which a woman may not remarry after being widowed or divorced

118

Commandments of Islam[1], and an expedient that leads to vile deeds, along with the fact that it does not restrict divorce at all. Its violation to Islam is illustrated in the evidences presented previously, which confirm that the divorce is in the hands of the husband, and therefore, disregarding those Divine texts is a rejection of the Islamic Command.

It leads to serious social heinous acts; the husband may divorce his wife an irrevocable divorce, but the judge does not sign for it, and after a period, they may reconcile, and so they might live intimately together under the pretext that the judge has not ruled the divorce, and this type relationship is pure adultery in Islam, May Allah forbid.

And in case that the husband divorces his wife, and presents his case to the judge, they (husband and wife) are compelled to reveal to the judge their personal affairs (not known to the public), and so they might likely use all kinds of lies, treachery and slander in an attempt to convince the judge to issue the divorce. The judge himself is not infallible from inclining to his desires or to his goals.

However, if the judge is not convinced with the reasons presented to him, which call for divorce, then what is the fate of the married couple? Do they stay married? Or do they remain "suspended"? So one can estimate the damage that arrises from both assumptions. As for the fact that it does not lessen the problem of divorce, one

---

[1] refer to the fatwa included in the book "The rights of the husband and wife" by Shiekh abu Al-A'la Al-Mawdudi

can look at the examples of America or Germany, who set the matter of divorce in the hands of the judge, yet still they have the highest rate of divorce in the world!

Note: Whatever has been mentioned above does not change the fact that there are men who oppress and treat their wives unjustly by exploiting that solemn right in the worst manner possible, because every system in the world is liable to be used wrongly, and every man of authority is likely to abuse it, if he is ill-natured or has weak faith. But still, it is inconceivable that a good system like (the Islamic one) should be abrogated just because of some people who have abused it.

Islam's first pillar of faith is established upon the awareness of the Muslim intentions, righteousness and duties to God; and in order to achieve that, it followed the most appropriate of all paths. Furthermore, if we refer to the theory of preponderance between the Masalih and Mafasid[1], we would find that when we look into the benefits gained in granting man the right of divorce in his hands, compared to the mischief suffered when denying him that right, the benefits clearly outweigh the mischief, and this is quite sufficient for its prevalence.

---

[1] Masalih: (pl.of maslaha) consideration of public interest. Mafasid (pl. of mafsada); evil, namely anything which violates the five essential values: Religion, Life, Intellect, Lineage and Property.

Among the differences: The condition that the Khalifah[1] should be a male

It has been confirmed in Sahih Al-Bukhari and others, on the authority of Abu Bakrah ﷺ that when the Prophet was informed that the Persians had crowned the daughter of Khosrau as their ruler, he ﷺ said: "Such people when ruled by a lady will never be successful", so this is a text that prohibits the election of a woman for the position of Khilafah, and that there is no success for those governed by a woman. This command (prohibition) applies to rules in the general (eg. the state presidency), and any other serious position (in terms) of responsibility. The majority of scholars have agreed that a woman may be a guardian of children and those who are legally incompetent; she could also be an attorney to any group of people with regards to managing their finance and conducting their affairs; she could be a witness in other that serious (bloody) crimes, provided that there was also a man (present) with her. But this is not related to the position of Islam with regarding the humanity of women; her dignity and competence; it is rather (closely) related to the interest of the nation, to the psychological nature of woman and to her social message.

The state ruler in Islam is not a symbolic figure of beauty who only signs documents! Rather, he is the leader of the Muslim society and its top thinker, prominent personality and spokesman. He possesses wide mandatory powers which have serious effects and outcomes:

---

[1] Muslim ruler.

He is the one who declares war on the enemies, and leads the state army on the battlefield; he could either agree to peace (or a truce) if it would be for the benefit of Islam, or decide to wage war and proceed with it, if it would be to the advantage and interest of the Muslims. His decisions are taken after consulting Ahl Al-Hal wal-'Aqd[1]; as Allah ﷻ has said: ❨**And consult with them about the matter**❩ Al-'Imran: 159.

He is the one who can deliver the Friday sermon in the mosque, leads people in Salat and sometimes settles disputes between litigants.

There is no doubt that these responsible duties do not conform with the psychological and sentimental constitution of a woman, and that her primary profession is to stay at home to concentrate on raising the next (future) generation, and to serve her husband; since she should not mix with men nor stay alone with anybody, foreign to her, for whatever reason.

A Woman has powerful feelings, which easily affect her, and (therefore) prevent her from using her intellect, resoluteness and power to overcome these aspects of tenderness and compassion.

How could she preach to people and lead them in Salat, when she is not even compelled to perform Salat Jumu'ah (Friday Prayer), and she cannot be an Imam for men in Salat? And how could correct worship be established, upon submission and voiding the mind of all

---

[1] "The people of loosing and binding" i.e. the scholars, leaders and army commanders who make binding decisions for the community.

distractions, if a woman stands as an adviser and an Imam.

And among the differences: the fact that Allah ﷻ has allowed men to marry up to four women at one time, if he knows (within himself) that he is capable of observing their rights, fairly, between them; as Allah ﷻ said: ❰Then marry other permissible women, two, three or four❱ An-Nisa': 3; as for women, it is not legal for her to be married to more than one man, for it is against (sound) nature, and because it leads to the mixing of lineage, and widespread mischief.

'Other regulations that distinguish between men and women

- The Prophet ﷺ said: "Whenever a man is alone with a woman, the devil is the third"[1].

- He ﷺ said: "A woman should not fast (optional fasts) except with her husband's permission if he is at home (staying with her)"[2].

- He ﷺ said: "Saying "Subhan Allah" is for men and clapping is for women"[3].

---

[1] Transmitted by Attirmidhi, and authenticated by Al-Albani.
[2] Transmitted by Al-Bukhari, Muslim and Imam Ahmad.
[3] Transmitted by Al-Bukhari. (If something happens in the prayer, the men praying (behind the Imam can invite the attention of the Imam by saying "Subhan Allah". And women by clapping their hands).

- He ﷺ said: "Shaving is not a duty laid on women; yet only clipping of the hair is incumbent on them"[1]. i.e. after the breakup from Haram in Hajj.

- He ﷺ said: "Had it been permissible that a person may prostrate himself before another, I would have ordered that a wife should prostrate herself before her husband"[2].

- He ﷺ said: "The best rows for women are the last ones and the worst ones for them are the first ones"[3]; "The best Salat for women is inside their homes"[4]; "The Friday prayer in congregation is a necessary duty for every Muslim, with four exceptions" and he mentioned women among them"[5].

Finally:

There is no doubt that this set of differences between men and women shows how far the Islamic system is adapted to the real life, and that whoever rejects these wise social principles, inevitably drifts from the bond of Islam, and eventually worships his desires (and Taghut).

---

[1] Transmitted by Abu Dawud, on the authority of Ibn 'Abbas ﷺ
[2] Transmitted by Attirmidhi, on the authority of Abu Hurairah; and Imam Ahmed, on the authority of Mu'adh; and Al-Hakim, on the authority of Buraidah. It was authenticated by Al-Albani.
[3] Transmitted by Muslim, on the authority of Abu Hurairah ﷺ.
[4] Transmitted by Attabarani, on the authority of Umm Salamah ﷺ, and authenticated by Al-Albani.
[5] Transmitted by Abu Dawud and Al-Hakim.

These Divine Legislations were not revealed to be kept only on paper, nor were they presented to people so they could examine how beneficial they are, and the possibility of implementing them. Rather, they were legislated to be practiced in a real world, that is affected by them; and any defect in observing them (i.e. believing in some and disbelieving in others) leads to an everlasting life of hardship and misery:

❲All those who follow My guidance will not go astray and will not be miserable. But if anyone turns away from My Reminder, his life will be a dark and narrow one, and on the Day of Rising, We will gather him blind. He will say; "My Lord, why have you gathered me blind when before I was able to see?" He will say: "Just as Our Signs came to you and you forgot them, in the same way you are forgotten today". That is how We repay anyone that is profligate, and does not have faith (Iman) in the signs of his Lord, and the punishment of the Hereafter is much harsher and longer lasting❳ Ta-Ha: 123-127.

125

TEN FRIGHTENNING THINGS FOR WOMEN

ABU MARYAM MAJDI FATHI AL-SYED

WISDOM OF THE WISE

ABDULAZIZ IBN NASIR AL-JALIL & BAHA ADDIN IBN FATAH AQEEL

THE RETURN OF

HIJAAB

PART III

عنصر

بلا

DR. MUHAMMED IBN AHMED IBN ISMAIL